4-30M-1

$3.95
LB

Bullfighter

Lady Bullfighter

by Patricia McCormick

Illustrated with Photographs

This is the courageous story of a pretty American girl who dared to become a bullfighter. Rich with brilliant accounts of the drama and panoply of the bull ring, it tells of Patricia McCormick's fascination for the running of the bulls and the peculiar sense of excitement she derives from the classic simplicity and grace of the *corrida*. A demonstration of perseverance and determination, *Lady Bullfighter* is a stirring book about a woman who invaded a man's world and achieved success.

Patricia McCormick, who has many times been awarded ears and tails for her performances, has also suffered painful gorings. Her courage, which prompts her to stand steadfastly before a charging bull, is at once the source of her brilliance and her *cornadas*. A

erself for a pass
ıy from the bull
ted. In this way
erous and artis-
ated. Miss Mc-
s fear, has on
ssed the bull so
the bull, bleed-
as smeared her
h his blood.
rich in the ele-
the *matadora*,
n sun casting
l, the grace of
of the *manole-
ment of truth,
ll. But there is
k — here the
centerpiece in
nely feminine

ho hails from Texas, has been fighting bulls for several years. She has attended the University of Texas and Texas Western. At present she is in Mexico studying under her tutor, Alejandro del Hierro.

Line Drawings by the Author

Patricia McCormick

Lady Bullfighter

The Autobiography of the
North American Matador

Illustrated with Photographs

Henry Holt and Company · New York

In Canada, George J. McLeod, Ltd.

First Edition

Library of Congress Catalog Card Number: 54-10526

Printed in the United States of America

To

Mother and Dad

Who were my first patrons

Preface

One of the few amusing incidents in the Tijuana hospital, where I was recovering from a goring, was the suggestion that I write a book about my career as a matador. That career was a little more than a couple of years old at the time, and I found it hard to take the idea seriously.

"Wait another five or ten years," I said when my teacher joined in demanding that I tell my story. "Then I'll know whether or not I know enough to write a book about bullfighting."

"We don't expect a textbook on the art and science of *tauromaquia*," they said. "We just want the story of a North American girl who gave up most of the things a college girl expects from life to pursue an ideal foreign to most women anywhere and to all but a handful of non-Latin men."

My maestro insisted, and since he demands obedience in everything, I agreed—with misgivings.

So here it is. I must hasten to acknowledge that much of what I say about bullfighting must be credited to others. My maestro, Alejandro del Hierro, is responsible, of course, for most of my knowledge of the science and art, for constant training and coaching, in and out of the bull ring, and for passing along to me knowledge that cannot be written or spoken, but only inferred or gained by the association of teacher and pupil. How to acknowledge countless other debts is beyond me, for I have learned by reading and by watching and listening to experts, those matadors who have reached the top in their profession. To all of these I offer humble thanks, realizing my debt to them and to the writings about them and their art.

If one traces his sources back far enough, he can claim little for his own in any field, it seems to me. What *is* mine is the aspiration to reach the top category attained by the best men of the profession—an aspiration driven by the restless need to satisfy something in me that seeks to discover in this art the meaning of my life.

P.McC.

Contents

ix

Lady Bullfighter

One

Sunny Sunday

Afternoon

"Are the bulls big?" I ask Martín, who is lacing my soft Spanish leggings.

"Big enough," he answers and immediately makes some comment on the stitched design of the leggings. Martín, who is my sword handler, does not like to talk about the bulls just before I am to fight them. Martín is a worrier.

"They'd better be," I say, a little resentful that Martín might be happier if the animals I am to meet were tame cows with blunt horns instead of bulls of caste, with centuries of breeding to fit them for this afternoon's spectacle. I get more satisfaction from a fight if the bulls are large.

All morning I have been impatient for the time to pass; now that there is not a full hour left, I wouldn't mind prolonging time a little, until I remember that I have something new to wear in the ring today, if Alejandro will let me: a *calanes* hat from Spain that Mariano has brought me. It is of blue velvet and copied from the time of Goya. I am about to mention it to Martín when I hear a low familiar whistle outside my door, followed by a rhythmic knock.

Martín gets up and opens the door for Alejandro. I have a moment of envy as he appears in his glittering *traje de luces* (suit of lights), the ancient costume of the *torero*, little changed from the days when Spanish noblemen were the principal fighters of bulls. As he smiles confidently at me, searching, I know, for signs of anxiety on my part, I have a momentary regret that I am a woman and wear the comparatively drab costume of the Andalusian countryman. And I remember that, except for the human animal, it is the male who wears colorful plumage and that it is primarily a man's world in which I will perform this afternoon.

"How goes it?" Alejandro asks in Spanish as he drapes his beautiful parade cape over a chair. He is sweating in his confining satin, heavy with embroidery and sequins.

"Fine," I answer, trying to add a reassuring smile.

It is always about the same, and the searching and answering or evasive glances mean more than the words. We know what is ahead: that all fighting bulls have horns; that some are big and brave and some small and difficult; that I must remember much that has not yet become instinctive with me; and that under the best of circumstances a meeting of *torero* and bull does not always result in drama that is emotional and artistic.

Martín finishes lacing the leggings. He checks the little silver ornaments sewn into the buttonholes of the wide cuffs of my Andalusian pants and I stand up to survey the result in the mirror. I tuck in the lace-frilled shirt, and Alejandro holds up the Spanish leather chaps with the stitched figure work on them and ties them onto me, wrapping the long lacings around my waist so that the fringed tassels hang down in front. The chaps flare out at the bottom over the leggings and below my trousers. Martín holds the short jacket, and when that is on and the filigree ornament is fixed at the shirt collar in place of a tie, there is nothing left but to don my hat— the broad-brimmed Córdoban or the little blue new one from Madrid. I hold up the blue questioningly.

"Bueno," Alejandro says, deferring in this moment to my femininity, and I perch it rakishly on my head.

The moment of departure for the plaza has come. It is always significant, for it is the time when I leave the solitude that has been mine for the irrevocable march toward the meeting with the bulls and triumph or failure. I do not think much about the possibility of gorings —perhaps because I am young and ambitious for achievement—but I am very conscious of the possibility of making a fiasco of the afternoon, and while my life has been a march toward my destiny of this particular afternoon, the sense of destiny is never quite so immediate as this moment of dressing and departure from my room for the ride to the arena.

I light the candle in front of the pictures of the Virgin Mary and Christ in the leather case on the dresser. A hurried prayer and I pick up my fuchsia-colored, raw-silk cape with the golden lining. I have no thought now of comparison with Alejandro's beautifully embroidered, satin parade cape. We leave the room, Martín carrying the tooled-leather sword case.

Strangely, it is now that I begin to feel lonely. While I am alone in my room those long hours from breakfast until this moment, I don't consider myself lonely. I have my thoughts, and perhaps my anxieties, but I am not so lonely as when I emerge from the solitude of the room into the festive gaiety of the public on an afternoon of a *corrida de toros* (running of the bulls). Now I have to be two persons—the one I am inside, the flame that makes me do this thing which is strange for a woman and for an Anglo-Saxon, and another person who smiles at people and walks erect and guards the inside person and the flame and the feelings.

I try not to blink as flash bulbs glare. I nod at those who call out my name. I autograph tickets or pictures as gracefully as though I were merely going out to dinner. I am conscious of the holiday feeling all about me, and the "outside me" acts as though I were a part of it; the "inside me" feels like a priest or a sacrificial goat or, perhaps better, a vestal virgin going to the altar in an ancient rite of blood offering for the sake of all these well-wishers.

Truly, in a sense, the brave festival at its best is a sacrifice in which the crowd is shown that man can by art and skill and valor face, deal with courageously, and overcome death, man's greatest enemy, the unknown, inevitable victor over life. And all the time I'm apparently arrogant to prove to these people that death can be faced without fear, all the time I'm smiling and nodding, my mind is on what lies ahead of me. I don't think it is fear that trembles in my stomach, but there is a welling up of anxiety, if for no more than that I don't perform well this afternoon and don't give these people who are going to see me against the bull the satisfaction they seek. This is often followed by a feeling of indifference, if not of rebellion, against what is expected of me. For the real anxiety is perhaps a little lack of confidence that I will measure up to my ideals and perform the ritual according to the high standards set for it by the masters of the art. For (let us get this straight) I do not consider bull-fighting a sport; it is an art, a science, and a ritual, and like any other art it can be good, bad, or great, according to set rules and the ability of the matador to perform within those rules.

When we are in the car, we are again isolated somewhat, like an island in a sea of cars, all bound for the plaza. The glitter of Alejandro's suit now and then attracts attention as the car slows or stops for a signal. Now and then we are recognized, and someone shouts, *"¡Suerte!"* (luck), or *"¡Ole!"* It is a procession that might be bound for a football game or an opera. Finally the bowl of the plaza looms up and the driver makes his way through the crowds to the gate we are to enter.

The bundle of working capes and the smaller, scarlet *muletas* are unloaded. The door is opened cautiously until we are recognized, and then we step inside and go straight to the patio of the *cuadrillas*. (Each matador has a *cuadrilla*—a team of three *banderilleros* who assist him and place barbed, decorated sticks, called *banderillas*, in the bull's shoulders—and two mounted picadors.)

5

Here too are those who want autographs and some friends with more personal wishes for a good afternoon. There are the picadors trying their horses, and the servants of the ring performing various chores.

There are other *toreros* in the tunnel under the stands leading to the patio where we will form for the parade into the ring. I nod to those I know and move down the tunnel toward the light that comes in over the *cuadrilla* gate. I ignore, as though it were not there, the door on one side marked "Infirmary" and glance at the door opposite, which leads to the little chapel, to see that it is not occupied.

In the chapel I am alone again. I drop the "outer me" and try to be completely honest with myself. I kneel at the prayer desk before the image of the Virgin of Guadalupe, the special patroness of all Mexican bullfighters. To one side there is a picture of the Virgin of La Macarena, the patroness of all bullfighters. There are flowers at their feet and candles burning before them. I remember the secret vow I have made to Guadalupe and pray for the protection of all the others who will face the bulls this afternoon.

I never pray for protection in any form for myself. That is my responsibility. Nor do I pray about the weather or that the bulls will be good. I have to fight as well as I can and defend myself regardless of the type of bulls. All I ask of the Virgin is that she will be with me.

I have a special prayer that those matadors who have gone before me will guide me, show my wrists what to do, and help me to learn and gain wisdom in my profession; that each *corrida* will increase my knowledge, regardless of the qualities of the bulls I fight.

Outside the chapel I am detained again by well-wishers and autograph seekers, but I go as quickly as possible to the *cuadrilla* gate where Alejandro and my *banderilleros*, Pancho Balderas and Mariano Rivera, stand, smoking and talking. They smile when I come, smiles of reassurance and encouragement, and wish me well, knowing—as the others do not—what they are wishing and why.

The two matadors who will alternate with me come to the gate. We greet each other formally, each thinking his own thoughts, and perhaps each, humanly, hoping he will outperform the others. Despite studied nonchalance, the smiles and careless talk among the *cuadrillas*, anxiety reigns here. You can smell it, and I fervently wish the hour would come and the gates open for the parade across the sands. Once that happens, there is no more waiting; a bullfight moves according to schedule, however varied each one may be.

"Let's get this thing going," I repeat to myself.

As though catching my impatience, the crowd overhead in the sunny section of the ring starts to chant, " '*La Macarena*,' " " '*La Macarena*,' " over and over, demanding the ancient song that immediately precedes every bullfight.

As though an answer to prayer, as well as prayer in itself, the trumpets high above the ring and across from our gate announce the solemn strains. The gates open, and behind me the *cuadrillas* line up, giving a last tuck to their parade capes and pushing their hats down over their eyes. The sun is glaring as we face it. It sparkles off the golden suits of the men. We listen to the song, and I remember all the great matadors who have heard it before marching to the undercurrent of the drums to their destinies. The song ends in a burst of applause and the *alguacil* (bailiff) rides his beautiful trick horse across the sand to bow before the authority in his box and then backs the horse, retracing his steps, to the *cuadrilla* gate to lead the procession.

A strange thought comes to me, incongruous but with a touch of ironic humor that relieves the strain, as I look out at the crowd:

"We are gathered here today, brethren, to witness . . ." But I've never gone farther than that. I've never found the words I've wanted to finish with, but I have wondered just why some of them do come.

The band strikes up another *paso doble* (two-step). I look to the sky, cross myself, and glance at the matadors on either side of me. They defer to me to start, and I march out into the ring, the others falling in step, our *cuadrillas* in file behind us, the mounted picadors last, before the gayly harnessed mules and the ring servants.

I know that by contrast with the men in their glittering suits of lights I am not glamorous, but I walk straight, head up and with an easy swing, my cape carried simply over my left arm. As we get farther into the ring, individual faces on the shady side become recognizable. To these I can smile more personally. At the *barrera* (barrier) we stop below the president's box and bow. Then we step behind the barrier, the men to pass capes up to be draped before honored guests or favorites. Mine is the one I shall use, and I have the first bull. When all the men are in the *callejón* (the alley that circles the ring, separating the barrera from the wall below the first rows of seats), I take my place in front of the opening in the *barrera* we have just come through, behind the *burladero* (shield), which stands just far enough in front of the barrier to permit a man to slide between them into the *callejón* and too close to permit the bull to enter. Alejandro moves in beside me, and I see that Pancho and Mariano have gone to other *burla-deros* before other narrow entrances to the *callejón* from the ring. The ring servants are grooming the sand in the ring, smoothing the path of the parade.

A name goes up over the door of the tunnel from which the bulls will emerge, and I forget everything in my anxiety to see what kind of a *toro* will come out, and how. The ring is now completely empty.

A bugle breaks the silence and the tunnel door opens. There is complete silence again in the ring and in the seats above it, an expectant quiet as before a storm, as all eyes look at the blackness the open door has exposed. My anxiety increases to the point of exasperation when nothing comes from that darkness. What is the trouble? Have the men fumbled the inner gates? Could it be that the bull does not want to venture into the brilliant sun to challenge anything he meets? I think of the difficult and cowardly bulls I have met before, bulls which would not charge frankly, permitting good work; bulls which stood completely on the defensive so that I have had to carry the fight to them on every pass. It is the brave bull, the bull which challenges everything in his way, which permits a good fight.

Mariano slips out from behind the *burladero* near the tunnel gate and peeks into the dark passage. I see

9

him flick his cape enticingly in the sun before the blackness. He does this three or four times before the bull comes out, not charging defiantly, but rather cautiously, investigating. When Mariano slips back into the *callejón*, the bull stands looking about the ring. Some of the audience laugh. I hear someone call out, "Ferdinand," but it is no joke to me or to the members of my *cuadrilla*.

Across the ring Pancho Balderas waves his cape and calls. The bull—not a large one—looks, takes a step or two toward the enticing cape, and halts, pawing the ground—usually the sign of bluff rather than a challenge or a desire to fight. Mariano has to lure him from the side, and finally they get him running, a few charges which stop short of the *burladero* behind which the capemen slip after displaying the lure.

"A *bicho* [a bug]!" Alejandro says with disgust, and he goes into the ring, shaking out his cape and calling to the bull. My mouth is still dry and no words come; I think of all the Americans in the stands who have come to see me, Americans who do not understand bullfighting and who will think this bull and the little I can do with him represents what the Spanish race calls the brave festival. And I try to think what I can do with him—if there is any way I can give him confidence in the cape and *muleta* so that he will charge, permitting artistic work.

Alejandro goes close to the bull and flicks the cape right under his nose. The bull hooks at it with his right horn and, as Alejandro withdraws the cape a little, goes after it, hooking, trying to catch it. Finally Alejandro is able to zigzag backward across the ring, dragging the cape after him on the ground, the bull following, trying

10

to get it. He brings the bull close to my *burladero*. I go out into the ring and approach the bull, the cape open in front of me.

I shake the cape in front of him as he looks at me. I call to him, coaxingly, "Hey-hey, eh, eh, *bonito*. ¡*Mira*! ¡*Mira*! Ah-h-h!"

I have to step out firmly again and lightly shake the cape, still calling more sharply before he will attack. He passes, not charging hard but sort of hopping. I turn to cite him again, but I have to stamp my foot and flick the cape repeatedly before he comes, and I pass him on the other side, not suavely I know. I hastily search my knowledge for the best means to teach him to follow the cape and charge more frankly. I call again, this time "*Bicho*." He is not *bonito* (beautiful) at all, but a difficult animal who wants to wait rather than try to throw everyone out of the ring. I cannot do a good *remate* with him (a pass which turns and fixes a bull so that one can walk away from his horns). I can walk away from this one, all right, but there is no emotion, no appearance of dangerous contempt in my going, for the bull is not interested and everyone knows he has no intention of attacking or pursuing me.

Many of the people laugh. Perhaps some of the knowing ones understand my predicament. There are remarks from some of the North Americans that I can hear. Oh yes, they could kill the bull, all right! And of course the danger is all pretense—there is no danger. And if this is what all the publicity is about, I must have a good press agent.

I ignore the comments, still angered that I haven't a better animal or that I can't teach such a one to perform better, for a great matador can be skillful with a poor bull, even if artistry is impossible.

The horses, padded for protection and bearing the picadors, are in the ring, but the bull shows no interest in them and has to be coaxed to attack even after he has been lured close to one of them. The *pic*, well placed in the hump of his neck muscle near his shoulders, quickly discourages him and he runs away. Perhaps it is fortunate, for I am supposed to take him away from the horse in what is called a *quite* (kee-tay), and I know I could do little that is interesting with this animal, though I am still trying to decide what would interest him enough to make him fight.

While the *banderilleros* are trying to lure him close enough to be *pic*-ed again, he really tries to escape—even jumping the *barrera* into the *callejón*. The crowd roars with mirth as ring servants and *toreros* leap from what is supposed to be a protected alley into the arena itself. This is becoming a circus!

Gates are swung, blocking the alley and forcing the bull back into the ring as the trumpet sounds, ordering the horsemen out of the arena. The first act is over, and I go to the *barrera* in a sullen mood.

"But the beast is a coward," I hear a man argue, a man with a Spanish accent.

"Coward, hell," comes a Texas drawl, "He's smart!"

Pancho runs out, holding the pointed and gayly wrapped *banderillas* shoulder high, clacking their tips and calling to incite the bull to charge. Pancho is unprotected and alone in the ring, but the bull is hesitant. He finally starts, and Pancho runs a quarter circle across his path, but the bull stops short and hooks, and Pancho has to turn quickly and gets only one barb into the animal's hump. The crowd hoots—that part of it who do not know enough to realize that it is not Pancho's fault. "Watch his right side," Pancho says as he comes back into the *callejón.* The second pair go in, but not gracefully, and the third are practically planted from behind a standing bull. None of it is exciting in the ballet manner in which these good *banderilleros* perform when the bull is good.

I step again into the ring and take the scarlet, heart-shaped *muleta* and sword in my left hand in the traditional manner. I face the stands, looking up at the judge as I take off my hat—the routine request for permission to kill this bull. The judge nods his head and I hand the hat over the *barrera* to Martín; I will not dedicate such a bull to any friend or honored guest.

Alejandro has been standing near the bull, his cape in front of him, ready to hold or guide him to the terrain I wish.

"High passes," he says, "He favors the right. *Piton a piton* [horn to horn] with the cloth."

I go out and cite him for a *pase por alto* (high pass). He takes it, but as I raise the *muleta,* he fails to charge up and high as a fast bull would. He turns quickly, trying to hook. Then he just stands, refusing to charge the cloth no matter how I cite. I have to go close to him, offering myself as much as the *muleta.* I have to *trastear* (work him with the *muleta*) from horn to horn, turning his head this way and that until he charges, but even when he does he isn't very anxious. I have difficulty keeping him interested in the cloth and making him turn and recharge. I literally have to chase him! I decide to kill him quickly without dragging it out any longer.

When I go to the *barrera* for the killing sword, Alejandro warns me again that he's bad to the right. That is the horn I have to clear as I go in with the sword to kill, and a bull who doesn't follow the *muleta* well may not follow it to the left, permitting me to clear his right horn.

I *trastear* him again a few times and line him up, feet together and head fairly low. I raise the sword as I profile to him, *muleta* furled in front of my legs. I sight along the sword toward the one spot, about as big as a dollar and high on the bull's shoulders, where the sword can pass between the blades and honestly kill him. As I come to his head I cross the *muleta*, still low, to my right, as I reach over to shove in the sword. But at that moment he hooks, and the sword hits bone that feels hard as granite. His right horn jerks up between my legs, tossing me into the air. I fall onto his back and roll off onto the ground, hardly conscious of the great gasp of the crowd. Alejandro is at once before the bull with his cape and someone is trying to help me up. But I am mad, so mad at the stubborn little creature who won't fight or charge that I push away my helper, telling him to get out. Disheveled, I look for my sword. I still have the *muleta* in my left hand.

No one who knows bullfighting is going to be too critical of a bullfighter who doesn't go clear in over the horns of a bull who will not charge, but I am determined to kill this animal as cleanly and honorably as if he were a great, brave, fighting bull.

I *trastear* him again, talking to him sharply. Then I square him for another try. I watch his head carefully to be sure he is focused on the *muleta*. I profile and go in again over his horn. I cross the *muleta* over to his left, and this time the sword enters as though into butter and I hunch myself over the lowered horn as he turns away after the cloth. He staggers around a couple of times and falls to his knees. There is an ovation, probably because I have gone in clean a second time, after being tossed. I bow to the judge and go behind the barrier to ask Alejandro what I could have done better.

"Don't worry about him, he's dead," Alejandro says easily. "He was the worst of the lot. Because of that he was paired with the best—that's your next bull."

"He'd better be the best," I growl.

Martín brushes me off as I wipe my face with a towel. The mules drag the bull from the ring and the sand is smoothed again for the next fight. I ignore the remarks of some of the North Americans in the seats above me who consider themselves very tolerant for coming to witness a bullfight in spite of their prejudices. I never get hot-headed over remarks that to a sincere *torero* can only sound insulting, for they spring from ignorance. I can even pity those who see no difference between the conduct of the *Fiesta Brava* and the actions in a slaughter pen. The standard I really have to measure up to is my own.

I have found no self-satisfaction with this bull. Surely there was little in the fight to give me triumph over the other two who may well do better with their bulls. But my maestro seems satisfied, so I can only wait my next turn and try to do better. If the bull is superior, perhaps I can give an artistic and emotional performance; if he is not, I must try to gradually bring him around to fighting as I wish, and then perhaps we can do interesting work.

The second bull of the afternoon comes out bravely, though he is not of the best. He charges well, and the crowd becomes less amused and more interested. I even win *oles* when my turn comes to make the *quite*—to take the bull away from the horse and picador after the *pic* has been planted for the second time in his shoulders. The rest of the second fight goes smoothly enough, if not spectacularly, and the young man gets an ovation and a tour of the ring.

The third bull really roars out and challenges everything offered to him. Alejandro whispers to me that he is the best of the two bulls drawn by the third matador for his lot; that he, being the last fighter to appear, wants to be sure he has his good bull before the crowd tires and starts for the exits. I am exhilarated when I pass him in my *quite*; he restores my confidence in my ability to handle bulls smoothly. Again the stimulating *oles,* and enough applause to bring the band on with a *Diana,* the music played for a good performance. The young matador is out to take all the honors; he is reckless and is bumped around, even going off his feet, but he is brave and eager. His performance is partially spoiled by his difficulty in killing, but I withhold conscious judgment, since I had to go in twice with my first, and I have another coming—now.

"Oh, Holy Virgin, that I will have the knowledge! That he will be brave, strong and honest!"

He is all of that, though I don't have time to be prayerfully thankful until it is all over. Just grateful inside myself.

He roars to the center of the empty ring, and throws his head up challengingly, master of all he surveys. A cape flicks out from behind a shield. He charges fast, head down, and the cape is moved along the barrier and withdrawn as he reaches it. He splinters the wood and searches for the cape before turning, challengingly, back to survey the ring again. Another cape flicks from another shield. He races after it, but this time looks to see where the cape goes.

He follows the cape well, too, in the first running. I see that he is frank and brave and that he also favors his right side a little. When I go out for the first time with him I can do good *veronicas*, each pass linked to the other; and I finish with a *remate* that leaves him fixed, facing me. I turn proudly—as proud of him as of myself—my back to him and his horns, and salute the crowd. There is applause and music.

He lifts up the first horse and picador onto his horns in spite of the punishing *pic*, and I have to take him away from horse and man. He goes past me so beautifully that I forget everything but that bull, and the movements come naturally and instinctively while something inside of me swells, like the bursting open of doors and windows of a room that has been suffocatingly close. The stretch of freedom.

I hate to leave the beautiful *toro* when I have placed him for the next picador. He proves his merit by attacking the second horseman as bravely as the first, despite the gash in his crest from the first *pic*. And he charges the third as valiantly, and has to be brought off again to save the horse and rider.

The *banderillas* are well placed in a matter of seconds, it seems to me, and Alejandro is telling me to be calm as I take the *muleta* and sword for the final act and go before the judge's box for permission.

I offer the pass of death and the brave beast charges, going high off his fore legs as I lift the *muleta* straight up. I pass him with the right hand, the *muleta* extended by the sword, even taking him from behind in this fashion, and then I hold the sword alone in my right hand and with the left offer the *muleta*, small by comparison, in the classic low, *natural* pass. He takes it beautifully and I link others to it, finally passing him from behind, high up under my armpit, his horn just grazing my jacket over my ribs. I could keep this up all day! I am in no hurry to kill, you lovely, brave beast. But I must, before you learn how to kill me. I know you will die at the height of your courage, trying to fathom the illusive cloth that you can't get your horns into, searching for the real enemy you would destroy.

When I first line him up for the kill, he charges before I can go in, and I have to pass him again. I line him up and this time I profile more quickly, furl the *muleta* and look down my sword, over the horns to the spot the sword must enter. I step forward, crossing my left arm with the cloth low and over to my right. For an instant I am against the bull's head, between the horns as the sword sinks in up to the hilt. I feel myself lifted a little as I clear the horn and he turns into the *muleta*. I feel his whole body go by me before he stops, tries another step and falls to his knees.

A great roar engulfs the arena. I am still looking down at the beautiful animal I have killed when Alejandro comes over, removes the sword, and tells me it was good.

I walk over in front of the judge's box. Applause and shouts reverberate all around, almost drowning out the music of the band. The judge holds up one finger and Pancho hands me an ear he has cut from the bull. I bow and hold the ear aloft in my right hand, but the crowd is not satisfied. The yelling increases and the whole arena seems a flutter of white handkerchiefs. The judge grants me another ear and the crowd goes wild. I start to make a tour of the ring, Alejandro and Pancho behind me, trailing their capes. Hats, flowers, cigars, pens, and pencils shower down. I put a *charro* hat on my head and the crowd loves it. I toss back some of the objects and my *banderilleros* return the rest, except, perhaps, for cigars. I catch a bouquet of roses and hold it with the bull's ears in my right hand after sailing the *charro* hat back up into the stands. Then someone comes running and hands me the tail of the bull, and it seems pandemonium will break all bounds as the happy throng applauds. I am so elated that I forget my fatigue and walk around the ring as though with the sandals of Mercury. It is an hour of triumph for the bull as well. He too gets a tour of the ring before being dragged to the *arrastre*. He too gets his applause, because of his bravery and honesty, his true nobility. I have to make several tours before the crowd quiets enough so that the bugle announcing the next bull can be heard.

Back again in the *callejón* Martín, all smiles now, takes time from his cleaning of swords and folding of capes to pat me on the back. Martín is always glad and relieved when it is over.

19

The next matador stands behind the shield, biting his lower lip. I wish him well; I can afford to be magnanimous, having had my triumph. For me the last two bullfights of the afternoon are routine affairs which I see through the rosy hue of my success.

There is the hustle to the car when the last bull is dead, and again the photographers, the congratulations, and the need to sign autographs, though my hand is suddenly tired and the signatures are more like scrawls. Then the slow procession back through jammed streets to the hotel. The words of old-timers, *"En hora buena, Señorita,"* are particularly welcome when someone substitutes the word *"matadora"* for the *"señorita."* "A good hour, matador."

Then the solitude of the room again. The candle before the pictures of Christ and the Virgin still burns. I shall let it burn throughout the night. Now I offer my thanks as unselfishly as possible, forgetting the personal elation. Then I sink into a chair to rest a little before my shower. Martín orders tea sent up, and I realize how long it has been since I have had food and more than a swallow of water.

We discuss the fight until the tea is finished and my leggings are off. I am now almost too lazy to get up and undress and take a shower—a good, lazy, happy-tired feeling that I have acquitted myself well and another *corrida* is behind me. I am reluctant to leave my bullfighting clothes. I suddenly wonder if Alejandro will have anything to say about the fight when I ask him. I would like to have him dissect it, move by move. This rouses me and I get up. Martín goes, and I, alone with myself and my God, stand before the pictures on the dresser, thinking wordless thoughts.

This might be any Sunday afternoon during the season. Such an afternoon might be considered good, for with the last bull I have been able to fight well. There have been afternoons when things seemed to me to go so badly that all I have wanted to do afterward was crawl into my hotel room and cry. There have been times when even bad bruises have not seemed to hurt, my elation overriding any awareness of pain. And there was one afternoon when I ended in a hospital with a deep tunnel and a trajectory from that main wound in my leg.

Such is the "glamour" of being a "lady" bullfighter. It may be topped off with a pleasant dinner with friends, people coming to the table with congratulations and for autographs. The real glamour is not known by anyone but myself; it is the glow within if things have gone well and I have made the best of the bull and what I know of fighting him, artistically and emotionally, within the rules of the drama known as the *Fiesta Brava* —the Brave Festival.

259495

Two

Knights and Matadors

I saw my first bullfight in 1937 when I was seven years old.

My father, an engineer for an oil company, had taken Mother and me to Mexico during his vacation. I can still remember how excited I was when I learned we were going to Mexico, because I thought I would see real gypsies. I don't remember why I associated gypsies with Mexico, unless it was that I had heard of Spanish gypsies and knew that Mexico had a Spanish heritage; I suppose my association was derived from *Carmen,* or other music.

Perhaps it was that during previous vacation travel I

had seen the painting of "El Gallo," the great Spanish gypsy bullfighter who is still alive—"El Gallo" and a big black and white bull, fixed into one beautiful form with a scarlet cape. But I can't be certain I had seen this before that first bullfight. Anyway, I was thrilled that we were going into a land of romance, of singing, dancing, bullfighting, and adventure.

I did not see much that was gypsy (according to my imaginings) in Mexico City. But I was impressed by what I did see: cathedrals, sculpture, gardens, pyramids; it was stupendous to me, particularly in contrast to Arkansas City, Kansas, where we lived at the time.

And the bullfight! I remember that Mother had said we would not attend such a spectacle. I don't remember why she changed her mind, and I don't recall being particularly excited when it was decided that we would attend one. But once at the *corrida* I was caught up in the drama and excitement as I had never been before. The parade, the suits of the matadors, the bravery of men with live bulls, and the ovations given by the spectators —all of it was wonderful and meaningful to me.

I don't remember who the matadors were. I couldn't, of course, determine whether or not they performed well, except by the applause of the crowd. However, they were great to me. Their movements with the huge, black force of the bull were those of a beautiful, colorful dance. And even then the *corrida* seemed to me to be a dramatic unit. I had seen movies, but little opera or legitimate drama, but I thought this was what drama should be—living, vital, and real.

I was disappointed when I was told that only men could be matadors, and I questioned the statement to myself with characteristic stubbornness. To become a matador with the honor, grace, and bravery of such men seemed a worthy ambition. I did not wholly accept the idea that women could not aspire to such a career, though I did not argue about it.

I had always said that I would become an artist, when asked what I planned to be when I grew up. (At the age of three I had drawn so realistic a sketch of Dad in the bathroom that he had requested Mother to keep me out of that room while he was in it.) At that bullfight I felt that I had made a discovery: Here was art that was moving and not fixed on paper or in clay; art that flowed constantly for its brief life and left the mystery of art in the mind when it was out of sight. One could not say as of a painting, "The line is in such and such a place, the color here or there." It was formless while formed; it was living and pulsating.

My parents tried to divert my wide-eyed attention; they did not care for the spectacle and wished to leave the arena. I, in turn, was shocked and resistant to their efforts; how could they not enjoy it, how could they drag themselves away from the greatest thing we had ever seen? Their attitude only deepened the sense of mystery I came to associate with bullfighting in those young, very uninformed years. It came to embody—besides, or because of, the mystery—a great adventure, a chance for discovery, and a new aspect of my desire to be an artist, for I didn't think of it as a sport, even then.

Of course, as a child I didn't think of it in those terms, but I am describing the feelings I had as accurately as I can, looking back. It was more than merely the biggest thing I had seen; it was something in the order of a challenge. This was enhanced, of course, by the opposition, the antipathy toward it on my parents' part. I wanted to be alone after the fight, to think about it. My parents' remarks about the fight and the whole idea of bullfighting seemed almost sacrilegious to me. And then when we went off to Chapultepec and they exclaimed over the beauty there, I couldn't understand why they hadn't seen beauty at the plaza, and I resented their talk.

All this was recalled strongly sometime after our return to Arkansas City, when Mother and Father were telling friends about our visit to Mexico City. Of course the bullfight came up, with all the tones of disgust and disapproval. The friends concurred with my parents' opinions and proceeded to tell of one they had seen (the only one, of course) in which the bull had turned from the red cloth and had gored the matador. I remember that my feeling was one of anger that the man would have allowed the bull to get him. I suppose it was that he had provided added fuel for my elders' opinion about the barbarity of bullfighting. And I was mad at the bull. I was sure I would have been more stubborn than he and made him do as I wished, as though he were an insolent child, instead of an animal fighting as he had been bred to do.

This incident I had heard bothered me for a long time. I'd think about it before going to sleep at night, trying to figure out why the man was caught, how to keep the bull following the *muleta*—though I didn't know that term in those days. "Red cloth" was how I thought about it, and I knew that somehow the bull had to be attentive to it to make the fight successful. But there was also something about the tragedy for the man which was alluring and mysterious. I wondered if he had died, or if he had lost his courage if he lived, and whether or not he fought bulls again and if so, if he had learned how to keep the bull moving about him gracefully without getting caught.

It wasn't only at night that I thought about the *corrida*. During the day my feelings were less morbid. I actually played at being a matador. When Father mowed the lawn he had to be the bull, and I stood ahead of him with a large cloth and passed him under it, pirouetting for his return in as near an imitation of the matadors I could muster. The first time I played matador with the little boy who was my principal playmate in Arkansas City resulted in tragedy for me too. The "cloth" which had seemed handiest was an American flag on a stick, which made it easy to hold. It was quite a game—until Mother discovered it. At first I thought her exclamation of horror was because of the game, but before I was spanked, I learned that what had shocked her this time was the "barbaric use" to which I had put my country's emblem. The next time Mother interfered with this "passing," I was using a small tablecloth as a cape. After that I had to settle for an old blanket or my coat.

The dogs of the neighborhood made better bulls than my cats, who didn't "follow the cloth" very well. I always loved cats and had families of them—new ones coming and old ones to be buried, sadly and with funerals. I think I was closer to animals than to boys and girls; I had preferred animals to dolls and could have more fun with my cats than with playmates.

My first close chum was Marge Marks, after we moved to Edwardsville, Illinois, the same year, or within a year, of our visit to Mexico City and that bullfight, but I still had pets and loved animals. In fact, for years I was known in Edwardsville as the girl with the duck. This pet allowed me to dress him up, and I had Donald Duck jackets made for him. He followed me like a dog wherever I went. But he wasn't much good at playing bull to my matador.

It was in Edwardsville that I got an opportunity to personally test the idea that it is safer to remain still than to run if likely to be attacked by an animal. There was a spitz, called Teddy, who had the reputation of being a cat killer and of hating children. Most of the kids would run away whenever they saw him coming. I did too, the first time—until I remembered that I'd been told that a man is safer if he can dominate his fear enough to remain absolutely still than if he moves or runs. So the next time Teddy came down the street toward us, I didn't join in the flight, but stood still when he reached me. He seemed a little surprised, but only sniffed around, after his barking bluff, and went off.

My own dog, Laddie, was a mongrel. He looked like a toy police dog. I could pass him with part of an old blanket for a while, but he'd tire of the game and try to grab the cape between his teeth. Although I had pretty good luck training dogs, I still loved the independent cats who wouldn't have anything to do with my bullfighting or any other stunts.

It used to irk me when Mother asked if I were being kind to my animal friends. I loved them too much to hurt them, and I still do. I used to think Mother had more compassion for animals than for humans (I got spanked with everything from the hairbrush, pancake turner, paddle with ball attached, belts, and switches I had to cut myself). Dad liked to tell a story about Mother's making a scene on the street by kicking a man she thought was mistreating a police dog. She denies the kicking part.

I come naturally by my love and respect for animals, which some say make it hard to understand my career. My pets included every available sort, from reptiles up. I was afraid of no living thing and used to be popular with women swimmers who'd ask me to dive and catch, or chase away, water snakes and frogs. I loved swimming under water and trying to catch the quick-darting water life. Dad used to call me Mowgli, from Kipling's tale. Swimming was the best thing I could have done in athletics and, except for horseback riding, it was the sport I liked best. I would still like to do underwater deep-sea fish spearing.

I had learned horseback riding the summer before we moved to Edwardsville. I think I was still only seven years old, but I loved it and soon could put horses through the paces we all thought constituted good riding. From the first ride I wanted a horse of my own, but that would have been too large a pet to add to my collection. There was riding on an Indiana farm too, when we visited my grandfather. There was an uncle fourteen years younger than Dad who was always quite a hero or ideal to me. I used to imagine him in stories I'd make up and act out when alone.

Once he asked me to demonstrate bullfighting for some guests who had called. Some of them laughed and I wanted to leave the living room, but a cousin brought in an old evening cape and told me it was a real bull-

fighter's cape. I believed her for a long time and treas-
ured it.

There was a bull in a pasture on those Indiana visits
that always enticed me. Of course he was just a dairy
bull, and I didn't know then how different a breed the
fighting bull is from the other varieties, but he was a
bull. People were afraid of him and he was left pretty
much alone. I decided that, whatever else, he was very
brave, a bull which would never give up and could be
handled only by a brave person. I would play that he
was chasing me. I had to pit my intelligence against his.
In such play, fences did not deter him and I would swing
across a creek on a vine to outwit him. But he had as
much determination and courage as I had, in this fan-
tasy I'd half act out, and so it was a never-ending story;
he never quite got me and I never quite got him. Others
would enter into this play, which at night was in dreams
and during the day in imagination, but the bull would
always single out me, ignoring other characters in the
drama. It got to be so much a story, continually created
in my mind, that, while it seemed very real to me, I must
have recognized the fictional element, for I decided that
if only I had a camera I could film the story—one that
would surpass all the romances I'd seen in the picture
theaters.

Even when we went back home and I was in school
again, I'd dream about this bull or a mythical giant animal whose foundation in reality had been this dairy
creature. He followed me about nightly. Sometimes I'd
stand and pass him, using only my body as a feint; again
I'd seize a coat or large hat and save myself or others
from his charges. In the recurring dream the field was

like the Indiana pasture, but the locale was in Spain where gypsies danced and sang. Sometimes matadors rode up to this field, and somehow or other I'd contrive to sneak into their midst and before they could do anything I'd pass this bull with my coat. Even in the dreams I didn't have a cape. I wanted one badly but would always have to use some makeshift. An aunt had a real *banderilla,* but of course I couldn't have that.

There was a terror and a fascination about the bulls, whether the actual dairy creature or those of my dreams. I wasn't exactly afraid, nor did I hate them. I always had respect for them; even then they seemed to represent a force I had to meet and try to control. There was never any performing by me before a great audience; only in the dreams, where I'd join matadors, were there interested spectators to my performance with a bull. I wanted, and in the dreams always won, the respect of these men who were professionals. If there was any glamour connected with my play-acting or in the dreams, it was in the atmosphere I associated with bullfighting —the gypsies, the *flamenco* music, and dancing, which were all very gay. But the gypsies were not present in the sense of spectators at an event; I was one of them, an accepted person, but it was not for them I performed daring feats.

Later I wanted to do daring things to show the other children or the neighborhood that I had courage. This idea of courage had been fixed in my mind since I was five years old and had had an example of stoic acceptance given by a little Cherokee Indian boy in the dentist's chair. Mother had pointed him out to me while I was waiting, and protesting, against dental work of some nature. I couldn't let that little boy be braver than I was, and it made an impression I still remember.

I must have been a disappointment to Mother in many ways. She had me going to dancing school as early as six years old. I took ballet and tap, but I was only good at acrobatics, which didn't bother Dad. He always thought I should be good at athletics because of my long legs. Mother had wanted to be a dancer herself, and in her mind she had sort of transplanted that ambition to me. I never gave Dad anything to be proud of in the athletic field either, though. After we moved to St. Louis when I was twelve, I tried hard to make the softball team. I really enjoyed it, but with all my efforts—even to getting up early to catch an early bus—I just brought down the team's batting average and wound up as substitute left-fielder. In college I never particularly enjoyed watching football, though if I had a date who was good company and nice-looking, I enjoyed the spirit of it all and the fun before and after the game.

The greatest desire I ever had to be a good athlete was when I had a crush on my best friend Marge Marks' older brother, who was particularly good at basketball. I didn't seem to have feminine traits sufficient to interest him in even a second look, so I decided being athletic might do the trick. I can't remember just what I thought being athletic involved, but I went to the extreme opposite of femininity and used to sneak out of the house without washing my face. It worked, so far as getting his attention was concerned, for he made cracks about the girl who never washed her face and about high-water marks, and soon became interested in a girl more nearly his own age. I still had the crush when I left

Edwardsville and have never seen him since. I was, at times, jealous of Marge's friendship too. I was very conscious of my gangling arms and legs and pigtails. I remember sharing a book with a feminine girl in school, and comparing my paws, which seemed so large and knotty, to her soft, delicate hands.

I never had thought much about femininity until my crush on Jimmy Marks. When very young I often wished I were a boy, not so much because I wanted to be masculine as because, as a girl, I would be left out of too many things. When I climbed a hill and yelled like an Indian, I wanted to sound like an Indian brave, not a passive squaw, and I used to ask if I sounded like a man. I remember climbing a hill later and imagining I wore a winged helmet and carried shield and spear like any hero in a Wagnerian opera, though I hadn't seen an opera at the time. It was as a man I pretended to be a matador when I "passed" my playmates and dogs with a "cape."

Actually, when still in Arkansas City, I was dressed more as a boy than a little girl, it seemed to me. A barber cut my hair into a Dutch bob. I wore a Navy-type blue jacket and a short, blue skirt year in and year out, except in the snow when I wore boys' snow pants while other girls wore leggings and carried muffs. I guess I acted more like a boy too, getting into mischief. My parents were strict; I went to bed many a night without dinner. I always had duties too, which were supposed to be accomplished before I went out to play. I earned my allowance, which was ten cents a week, until I was in high school, when it jumped to fifty cents and finally to a dollar.

The only time I ever ran away from home, it wasn't rebellion or escape, but to follow two dogs, without any thought of where they were leading me. I was only three or four years old, and they led me to an old airport, the entrance to which was framed in an iron grating. When I tried to get back home, that grating was a sort of bearing, and no matter which way I started for home I always seemed to end up at that gate. I was gone a long time, and when a storm came up I became frightened. I remember actually resenting the thunder and lightning, as though they were defeating some purpose I had. I finally found my way to a neighbor's house, where apparently I felt enough relief from anxiety over being lost to play in a pool of rain water. They took me in, talked all kinds of baby talk, and changed me to dry clothes, which brought on my ever-ready resentment again, due to the fact that their little boy was present and I didn't think it proper that he should be. They took me to my parents' then, where I was met with a mixture of loving relief over being found and scolding for having left in the first place. My mother and father had called out the police to search for me. They tied me up for the rest of the summer.

But I never did mind playing alone; there were always plenty of imaginary people to share my play—gypsies, matadors, Indians, Knights of the Round Table, Robin Hood—all the characters of romance I'd read about, though I liked best to be read to or told about a story. It was the pictures I liked best. All these characters were grist for the mill of my young imagination. Whether alone with imaginary others or actually performing plays with my friends, I'd play hard. Marge and I thought the day a failure when we didn't skin at least one knee, and it was perfect when we were all banged up and in rags.

But I remember not enjoying things when I'd been sick or had a cold and had to spend days at a time in the house, looking out at others playing; in my solitary state I soon tired of imaginary company and would feel confined. It was purgatory. And when I finally did get out, it was wonderful. What to discover in all the space, what to do first? And I'd always find a stick or something to throw far, far, hoping I could make it disappear in the distance.

The most confining thing was, of course, school. I started when I was five and then was taken out for a year. I was always too impatient to sit long at anything. I'd rather tell my imagined stories than write them, and even with private art lessons the best part was walking to and from some landscape subject, though I always liked art and from the first grade on was considered good in art. Art was something that was always there, and as far back as I can remember I always answered "artist," when asked what I would be when I grew up. I remember being annoyed sometimes at the insistence that one should become something. I used to wonder, why not be interested in what one is now instead of what one might be in the future? It was always pretty much the interest of the moment with me, even after I decided that I would be a matador. When I had my friends, even in high school in Big Spring, Texas, charge my "cape" on some dusty road to or from school, I was a matador to myself.

But I always resented the quiet and confinement of

school. If not sitting quietly, we were standing in line for something. The small-windowed, fire-escaped buildings were like institutions. Depressing days. I spent a lot of extra time in those buildings for my sins, which usually were not paying attention but making up stories and using objects from my desk to act them out on its surface. The only study I really liked was drawing. It seems I always ended up in the last quarter of the class with the mischievous children. I was always one of the first to fall in spelling bees. I still can't spell. In one grade—I think it was the fourth—I spent most of the time in the cloakroom. I thought up tricks and pranks out of sheer boredom. But I never played hooky (I was afraid to) and had a dread of being late because of the fuss it involved, though after the first day of school each fall it seemed I just couldn't go back.

If I had any favorite studies aside from art, they were those parts of history and literature that dealt with discovery, daring, and romance, though even with these perhaps "study" is the wrong word, for I was never good at research. Once I had the story, the dates and perhaps the larger sense of historical importance were not my concern. I always loved the Greek and Roman myths and legends, and in the sixth grade I learned about King Arthur and his knights. They sort of replaced the mythological Greeks and the heroes of our own revolution, and for years I could mix knighthood with bullfighting in my play. Usually I was Sir Lancelot, sometimes Sir Gawain or Sir Percival. I never was very strong for Sir Galahad; somehow he seemed too nasty-nice. His weakness for Guinivere made Lancelot the favorite; he had discretion, but he also followed his impulses. Tennyson,

36

therefore, was a favorite above Shakespeare as my "studies" progressed from Achilles and Helen through Roland to more modern heroes.

By the eighth grade I was interested in the Civil War, and I still am. But it is evident that the conflicts, stories, and romance interested me more than the meaning of the events. I didn't ever study much at home. I'd dream about the stories or play my records, often in preference to meeting the gang.

High school in Big Spring, Texas, wasn't bad—at least it wasn't a big city. But I can't say I ever really enjoyed the school part, though Big Spring has been my home since 1943. But for steady living I'll take a Texas prairie any day to a city. Oh, I like the fast pace of the city for visits, but suburbs always seem depressing to me, as though everyone were lost, trapped, had given up whatever it was they had hoped for from life. I remember once in St. Louis thinking hard about this after the kids went into their houses in the afternoon, the blue lights from the windows, everything slowed down. House by house all more or less the same. I couldn't understand it. I always thought it must be different around the corner; there must be something better than the sameness and slowness and tiredness of the people. "Is that what growing up means?" I thought, and sincerely hoped not. Again, I'd wonder if I would have to live like that. I like an outlook from a home.

Today I prefer Taxco, San Miguel de Allende, and most of the picturesque smaller cities to Mexico City.

Dad often worried about my moods and because I was so much of a dreamer. He used to tell me that dreams were fine as long as I didn't let them master me. But I wondered how I could plot my own path if I didn't shoot for the stars. Dad knew I wasn't much of a student, and I guess he figured there wasn't much he could do about it. But he always encouraged me to read good books, the classics from which I derived so many of my acted-out stories. My parents still urge me to find time for good reading. And, of course, they approve of my love of art and music.

It was after we moved to Texas and I was in high school, that I really started to appreciate music. I had always liked it; the gypsy songs as well as popular arias from operas had long played a part in my private world of romance. But in Big Spring I started to study music more seriously. I began taking singing lessons. I would listen to symphony programs on the radio, and every Saturday afternoon I followed the Metropolitan Opera broadcasts from New York. Often I'd model heads of the various characters in the opera, fixing them on bodies made from pipe cleaners and arranging my own stage and props. I even thought up ideas for my own operas, often with matadors and gypsies as central characters.

Mother was more certain than ever that I would become an artist, though certainly not an artist of the bull ring. But I think she worried about my liking to be by myself so much. She used to urge me to ask friends to our house and to go to dances and parties with more enthusiasm. She thought me lax in a social sense and thought I should be more outgoing and less solitary in so many of my pleasures. I have always liked people, but I have never found it necessary to be with others most of the time. I do enjoy solitude, and it is fortunate that I do since I have had to be alone, or remain much to myself, while learning the art of the *Lidia*, bullfighting. But, perhaps, according to the rule books I should be more extroverted. Mother naturally wanted me to be what now is considered normal (though I've noticed ideas of "normal" change). My new interest in music permitted greater opportunities for solitary enjoyment. Not only the radio programs held me at home, but I started buying operatic records, which I would play over and over to myself. With the interest in opera, at least I was peopling my fantasies.

When it came time to decide what I was going to major in at college, I decided on music. Mother thought I should stick to art. I argued that opera was an art, an art that was fluid and fleeting, never static. Since Mother advised in such matters, rather than demanded, I went off to college as a music student.

Three

Why Not the Stars?

I'm afraid I looked forward to college as an adventure into life more than as a means of education. I hoped to get the education, but took that for granted. The education would come, but there was a choice in subjects, less restriction, and more room for discovery. It wasn't, as it was for some of my friends, freedom from parental authority or the social aspect of college life that lured me. I think "discovery" is the best word I can use to describe my feelings about going away to school.

Life has always seemed to me a field for finding out things—the meaning of life itself, why we do things and why we don't, a sort of search for the truth in life. I often felt that as a child, and in many ways I was still a child looking for something when I went to the University of Texas in the fall of 1948, and in some respects I still am. If growing up, becoming mature, means becoming set and feeling the certainty about values that so many adults seem to have, I don't know that I want to grow up. There doesn't seem to me to be very much that is absolute in living, and I can't believe that those who claim to be finally certain about life, whether in politics, society, or any other phase of living, are getting the most out of it.

I was reminded often enough that I should be vivacious, that I was too reserved and serious—perhaps too introspective—to be popular, though I was always ready for a good argument that might lead to finding out more about a subject. I wasn't what might be termed a goody-goody girl, but I never thought a continual search for a gay time was worth the effort. Trying to drink men students under the table never seemed a goal worth striving toward, and many of the sorority functions lacked appeal for me. I certainly don't mean to imply that drinking and parties were the prime interests of the majority of the students. There were other activities, and there were many serious students. I was neither socially adept nor a brilliant student, but I was trying to discover the meaning of living.

I hoped to find in music and drama satisfaction for the continuing urge to create and interpret. As when a child, I wanted to act in, be a part of, as well as plan and direct—if not actually originate—stories told through words, music, and dance. So I majored in voice in spite of Mother's warning. (I don't think she meant to pun when she said I was barking up the wrong tree.) But the dramatic aspects were hardly secondary; opera can be moving art, as the *corrida* is. The matador, sculpting with his cape, controlling the tremendous, living force of the bull, is a superior artist. I felt that music-drama was as close to that as I could come; though the hope that I might one day fight a live bull refused to be kept down.

I spent what spare money I had on records and books, rather than on clothes. *Flamenco* recordings from Spain, Haydn's First Symphony, and arias by Lily Pons started my collection of recordings. I didn't buy novels, but books on dramatics, stage lighting, Stanislavski, *Lilliom*, and one not connected with dramatic art, a book on deep-sea fishing. These formed the basis of my "library," aside from textbooks. I was afraid of books in English on bullfighting, afraid they would be prejudiced or, if not, at least wrong. I didn't even read *Death in the Afternoon* until later. I read parts of Tom Lea's *Brave Bulls* in the *Atlantic Monthly*, but in spite of my passion for the *corrida*, I didn't read the book at that time. I did study all the Spanish and Mexican bullfight magazines I could get hold of, and I tried without any luck to get a cape, which alarmed my family a little. I was supposed to have outgrown any childish interest in fighting bulls!

There were a few friends at the university who were interested in bullfighting as *aficionados*, and I enjoyed being with and talking to them, but for the most part my desires and ambitions along that line were private, though they were intensified after talking with those who had seen *corridas* and knew something about them. One young man would go down to the border to see them when he could get away from school long enough, and he used to bring me programs and magazines full of pictures taken in the arenas of Mexico, Spain, and South America.

I really entered upon my studies with zest, for I wanted to make the best of them. Perhaps it was that my heart was not in them sufficiently; anyway I soon discovered that the music courses were not meant for me. It is easy enough to say that I should have stuck to it; I tried just that for a year. There was no point in trying to kid myself, however, and after that first year I knew that I had better make a change without wasting more time. Staying at a thing may be good discipline, as I've found out with bullfighting practice, but it doesn't make sense if the practice is a fruitless effort to fit a round peg in a square hole. For one thing, I learned beyond any doubt that I did not have the voice for opera, and no patience on my part could make it of sufficient caliber. I decided to change my major to art (since they had no course on bullfighting), but I also sought the help of the counseling service in the effort to prevent a further waste of time.

The advisers approved of art as a proper course for me to undertake. But they also posed new questions in the process of giving me various tests. The doctor who discussed my aptitude test with me shook his head over my answers.

"Too ambitious," he said, as though scolding.

I guess I showed surprise.

"You must get over the idea of being best," he warned. "Look at me, I'm not the best."

He knew without my speaking that I was shocked. I didn't have to ask him why he wasn't one of the best. He saw the look on my face, and he blushed.

I was tired of being mediocre. By being best, I don't necessarily mean being top dog. Each star has its place in the heavens. We don't usually think of one as being better than another; all are celestial. Why shouldn't one try to be among the best? I still want no second run. If that is ambition, I'm ambitious—not for fame and glory, but to master what I have to do; to reach the *cumbre*, as they say in bullfighting, the summit. We don't think, as a rule, of one great matador being superior in every respect to another; Joselito, Belmonte, Gaona, Armillita— each is a star in his own right, but we wouldn't give up any one for another.

So I started my second year at the University of Texas as an art major—and on scholastic probation. I was able to get off probation, but I was not very happy in the art department and felt that I was getting nowhere, even if I was able to make passing grades. That aptitude doctor had not destroyed my ambition, if that is the word for wanting to succeed in whatever one undertakes. I enjoyed the art work, but felt that I would never get very far with the courses I had to take. I tried to be reasonable and not just an escapist; I came to the conclusion that I had better try studying art elsewhere and determine once and for all if an artistic career was possible for me. It wasn't so easy to determine as it had been with voice, in which lack of physical requirements seemed a final answer. So I wrote my folks about a change of schools.

Several other universities were suggested, from Wisconsin to the University of Southern California. I argued that most of these were either too big (as I felt the University of Texas was) or didn't seem to me to have superior art departments. I had already decided on Texas Western, in El Paso. Urbici Soler was teaching there, and I felt that if I took sculpture and life drawing from him I would soon discover whether or not I was an artist of sufficient merit to make a career of it. Also, though I carefully refrained from mentioning the fact, El Paso is right across the river from Juárez in Old Mexico. Juárez has a bull ring of "category" (standing) in Mexican bullfighting circles. I could easily see bullfights, and just perhaps get a chance to try fighting the bulls myself.

Soler turned the trick as far as getting my parents' permission to go to Texas Western was concerned—his presence on the faculty and the fact that the school is very much smaller than the University of Texas and, therefore, everything else being equal, better for an art major than one with many thousands of students and very large classes. So after three semesters at Austin I transferred to El Paso in February, 1950.

I could scarcely restrain my excitement at being but a few minutes from Mexico and a real *plaza de toros*, but I also resolved to do my best at school. I liked Soler, a Spaniard who told me he didn't like bullfights but went to them anyway. He said that the great Mexican Rodolfo Gaona had been his favorite until his retirement. Soler inspired me to do my best in sculpture and in life drawing, but I didn't do very well in the regular academic courses I also had to take. However, I earned passing grades in everything I studied at Texas Western that semester.

At the first opportunity I attended a bullfight in Juárez, the second one of my life, after more than a dozen years of dreaming about it. I went with three other girls from school. They had never seen a *corrida,* but one, the assistant to the dormitory mother, had read *Death in the Afternoon* and liked it. Hemingway had convinced her that there was much that was noble in the formal bullfight and that most Anglo-American opinions were little more than prejudice. She urged me to read his book, which I promised to do, though I was still curiously afraid that anything written by a North American —most of whom seemed to me to completely miss the significance of the *Fiesta Brava*—would at best be misleading.

The other girls knew nothing about the *corrida,* but they had open minds. I, of course, knew little that was valid, but I had studied the magazines of bullfighting published in Spain and Mexico by those who understood and appreciated the art, and a few Spanish books by or about matadors.

The *corrida* that Sunday afternoon was to have been a contest *mano a mano* (hand to hand) between a South American matador and a Mexican. I was very much disappointed. I did not know that there was little the matadors could have done to make the spectacle more brilliant, more nearly that of which I had dreamed since that first one in Mexico City. It was a very windy afternoon, and I have since learned, very personally, that wind is the worst enemy of the *corrida*—from the public's standpoint in that it prevents a good fight, and from the matador's for the added reason that it is extremely dangerous. A gust of wind may flip the cape out of control and guide the charging bull directly into the man. Wind is worse than rain and mud.

But, because the second *corrida* of my life was not all I had expected, it did not in any sense deter my ardor. I went again and again. Sometimes they were good and I felt that I had seen great art-drama that completely answered the requirements Aristotle demanded: the catharsis of the emotions.

Sometimes, usually with aspirants or young *novilleros,* I used to be impatient, an impatience that I carried home with me to my room in the dormitory, that they had not done all they could have, or that they should have had more valor or been more artistic or skillful, or that they did not make the best of a good bull. None of this impatience was generated by cockiness on my part that I could do better. Perhaps it was that I thought I would try harder; perhaps it came from sheer Yankee stubbornness. I felt something lacking in their performance, that the men weren't doing something they should do; that as long as the bulls charged, they should be fought to the utmost. At such times the actual fighting didn't seem to measure up to what I had read. I realized my own ignorance, and that all my reading would not make a bullfighter of me, and that I would probably feel differently with the real teachers of the art, the bulls themselves.

Even during that first semester at Texas Western I'd have quit school in a minute if I'd had half a chance to become a professional bullfighter, with a good teacher. I tried to be alert for any opportunity to learn from an expert. Someone in the dormitory told me about a girl in school who knew an old *banderillero* who had promised to teach her some passes. I phoned this girl, Julie Williams, and made a date for coffee between classes. She too wanted to be a bullfighter, but her family did not approve of her studying the art. But she did make a date for us with Bullido, the *banderillero*, and we went to his home in Juárez to meet him. Bullido asked me lots of questions in Spanish, most of which Julie had to translate though I had studied Spanish in high school. He told me about the fear of the horns and the jarring bumping of the bull. He talked of things other than courage, too, but all he could say only encouraged me more. He agreed to show me various passes the next Sunday, a red-letter day for me, April 2, 1950.

We drove to a gully in the Chihuahua countryside and Bullido showed us the *veronica*, the basic and essential *suerte* (pass) with the magenta and gold cape used in the first parts of the *corrida*. He showed me how to hold the cape, placing my hands and arms in the proper positions. He pointed out mistakes in my swinging, Julie translating all the time. She had her turn also. We returned to El Paso fired with enthusiasm. Fortunately, I didn't rush to the Dean's office and quit school at once. For there were to be none of the promised lessons with Bullido; Julie's mother forbade her going again. The last I heard of Julie Williams, she was a model in New York. I tried to get Bullido to carry on with me alone, but he refused, giving my poor Spanish as the reason.

Disappointment in being unable to take lessons from Bullido did not dampen my spirits for long. I had had a taste of swinging a cape, had been shown how to hold it, and the idea of becoming a bullfighter seemed to have a more concrete basis by that very fact. In my room

I practiced holding a cape as Bullido had shown me. When I returned to school from Easter vacation, I brought an old blanket with me. Soon I was trying to practice passes other than the *veronica*, passes which I would study in *La Lidia*, a bullfight magazine. I'd try all of them in front of the mirror, or in a little tower room of the dormitory, or outdoors. I didn't care who saw me or how much I was teased. I was accused of trying to start a new fad, of trying to be different, and of being just plain crazy. I didn't care, even when more sympathetic friends tried to persuade me that I could never become a bullfighter. All seemed to agree that I would outgrow it.

I soon gave up trying the passes illustrated in the magazines or that I saw during the *corridas* in Juárez, and stuck to the basic *veronica*. I thought the others would come more naturally if I could master that, and for the next year I did no pass but the *veronica*. I read everything I could about it from Spanish texts. It was slow, translating and trying to get the correct sense of the matter, but it was my chief interest. (I even flunked Spanish the next year. My teacher said he was very sorry since he understood the interest closest to my heart concerned the Spanish countries.)

Of course I wrote about my interests to my family. And during vacation I practiced at home and talked about the *corrida* constantly, and played *paso doble* and *flamenco* records until Mother told me I was taking it too seriously. I answered that it was the most serious thing in my life, and she said I should grow up, it was time I was becoming a lady, and so on. Once, when I was trying to show her a particularly colorful pass,

Mother stared at me a moment and then said that I must get over the idea of being a bullfighter; that I would have to choose between the bulls and my family. She was pretty serious, and I talked less about it at home, though I still practiced the *veronica* and played the music and dreamed of big bulls rushing past me, controlled by my cape.

When I returned to Texas Western in the fall, I was more certain than ever that I would have a try at bullfighting. I still had no certain plan to follow, but I knew that I wanted to be more than just an *aficionado,* as the fans, enthusiasts, and informed non-professionals are called. I knew too that I must have a good teacher; I did not want to repeat mistakes I had made in music. I could have taken lessons in manipulation of the cape and *muleta* from young *aficionados* or *novilleros.* But I was determined that if possible I would find a good teacher and learn once and for all whether or not I was pursuing the impossible.

An *aficionado* club was formed in El Paso, but I did not join. I attended many of their meetings and heard interesting talks by professionals and experts. I met many good friends who were more or less seriously interested in the art of bullfighting. I listened a lot to them. There was a young medic, Bill, who was stationed at Fort Bliss, who was one of the founders of the *aficionado* club, and Robert Ripley, who was its president, and others who were enthusiasts. I was more or less "going steady" with Tom, a young Easterner who claimed to be an *aficionado* and was anxious to face bulls in the ring himself, but he was less enthusiastic about my ambitions when they interfered with going to parties and dances.

I preferred reading Spanish books about **Belmonte,** "Armillita," and "Manolete" to spending time as many of the students did outside of their schoolwork. I stopped having coffee dates between classes and would practice instead, fighting bulls from class to class. At last I was seriously interested in studying, though my regular courses didn't go so well. I wanted to know why matadors used positions they did. I learned how Belmonte had followed the school of Pedro Romero, and the difference between the so-called Sevillian school and that of Ronda. I started keeping notebooks on famous fighters. I learned that Gaona was an *aficionado* before becoming a bullfighter, and how he had sought out and followed a good teacher.

I had learned that in music and art there are good and bad teachers, and I figured that it would be the same in bullfighting. A voice and career could be ruined with faulty instruction, and I did not want to make that mistake in bullfighting. I determined to follow the way of Gaona, if possible, and if a good teacher thought I might become a good fighter, put myself under his instruction and orders as completely as Gaona had.

Meanwhile I would learn all I could by myself and keep practicing as well as I could without instruction. In my room I would pick up a chair and hold it out as one would the *muleta* to strengthen my wrist and arm.

I tried to think through each pass I attempted, not just to strike a figure. The figure would grow with knowledge. I had learned in drama that an action should never be started without carrying or following through and figured this would hold true with the bulls too. Not having been raised with bulls, or in a *simpática* country, I had to compensate by using what I knew of related things.

But I didn't try to tear bullfighting to pieces, analyze it too much. I considered it a mystery and accepted it as such. I knew the basic thing was artistic, and tried to bring in Stanislavski's artistic conditioning—the freedom from tension and lack of self-consciousness. I felt that what I wanted to do was more important than myself. I overcame most of my natural shyness. I always told myself that someday all this effort would pay off. On windy days I would even wet my blanket with water, as the capes are watered to make them less subject to the wind's caprice. Often I felt alone in the world, lonely in the twilight, practicing while others were pursuing more normal pleasures. But it was not a melancholy lonesomeness.

I decided I couldn't afford to be away from the environs of Juárez during the summer vacation. My rather low grades made it seem perfectly reasonable to my folks that I stay on for summer school. Tom suspected the truth and did not approve; he had lost whatever enthusiasm he might have had for my desire to become a matadora. We had quite an argument before he left for the East. He accused me of wanting fame or notoriety or money. He said bullfighters were low in intelligence or they wouldn't be bullfighters. Naturally this angered me, who already idolized some of the famous matadors of history as well as of the present.

Tom had not approved of a picture that had been taken for the school magazine. Because I had talked bullfighting so much and constantly practiced with a cape, the editors had asked me to dress up in a matador's *traje de luces* and be photographed in the Juárez Plaza de Toros. They got me capes and a sword and took pictures in various poses, even one with a young *banderillero*, Jesús Gonzales, running with horns held out before him while I passed him with a cape.

What was important about that event was not known to the school editors or, I think, to anyone else. I dressed in silver and yellow *traje* and immediately became other than just a model posing for pictures. I felt as though I were in vestments of a sacred priesthood. I went into the little chapel of the Juárez ring where the matadors pray before the fight. I knelt before the Virgin of Guadalupe, holding the sword like a cross before me and prayed.

"I have taken the sword. Even though I can't speak your language, from this moment I dedicate myself, heart and soul, to becoming a true *espada* [swordsman]."

I prayed that She would help me, I didn't know how. I was emotional. I cried a little. I was so serious, and it was sort of like pleading with Mother. Guadalupe is the patroness of Mexico and of all Mexican bullfighters. I still consider myself dedicated, and from that moment nothing else mattered very much but getting started; the only thing that could have stopped me after that would have been the certainty that I could never be a success or being forced by a bull himself to forego a career as a matadora.

Nevertheless I was annoyed that the magazine called me matadora. I knew that I was far from being entitled to such distinction. One cannot be a bullfighter until he has fought bulls somewhere other than in dreams—let alone a "matadora," which implies high category. I knew there was more to it than just crossing a bridge to

Mexico and making a vow to the patron Virgin of that country. I had read enough of the histories of matadors to know that there was much hard work, though I never let myself think of possible danger. I knew the extremes to which many had gone to get recognition. I knew of the boys who had jumped into the ring during a fight to try to cape a bull, boys who had risked going onto the ranges where fighting bulls are raised to cape them by lantern light for practice. I knew I had far to go and that it might be years before I succeeded. I didn't care. I was willing to forego anything to achieve my goal.

The question of how I could meet a bull kept bobbing up in my mind. I wanted desperately to actually cite one and see what it would be like to try to pass him. I thought of all the cattle on Texas ranges, but I could think of no place where I could really find a bull even of beef or dairy variety, let alone one of the fighting breed. Then I heard that some of the boys of the *aficionado* club were going to the Juárez stockyards one Sunday morning to cape steers. I had a date with Frank King the Saturday before, and for once I tried all the feminine arts I could think of to get him to take me along. I was not very experienced in these wiles, since I'd been thinking only of bullfighting, but I finally overcame his protests that the others might object. He picked me up the next morning at ten o'clock and we joined Robert Ripley, Mr. Blanco, and a couple of others at the corrals in Juárez where steers, wild from the open ranges, awaited their fate.

The boys finally let me have a turn with one, though the steers were so wild you had to practically corner them to make them fight. Mine just wanted to toss his head with the wide horns. He tossed me a couple of times, too, but I finally got him to charge me and passed him successfully with a real cape. That was one of the most tremendous thrills of my life, passing that rangy steer! I almost cried for joy that I could do it—my conception of the *veronica* after a year of work with a blanket. I got him to charge the cape again and I did *gaoneras*, but the boys got worried and hauled me out of the corral. I was so happy I wanted to run off and be alone. They were all congratulating me and hoping the pictures they had taken would show how I had worked, but I remembered how it had been after that first fight in Mexico City, when I was seven. I hadn't wanted to talk or listen to my folks rave about the beauties of Chapultepec; I had just wanted to be alone and think about the bullfight. We all went for cokes and snacks, but I just sat very still, with a warm thrill inside me. Such joy is the greatest thing, makes it worthwhile going from one thing to another, joy to joy, even though each joy is momentary.

Mr. Blanco, who had let me use his cape, said I should become a professional.

"Never thought of it," I smiled, fibbing. Another said I should change my name and just start out; that my Scotch-Irish cognomen wouldn't work. I said I'd never do that. All tried to persuade me to join the *aficionado* club. But all I could think of was that steer I had passed!

Things happened rather fast after that. Perhaps it was the Virgin attending to my prayers, perhaps the fact that those boys who took me to the Juárez stockyards felt my determination and knew it was no whim. And some of it was due to the fact that the pictures they took turned out well and they showed them around.

I was introduced to Mr. Park Look, who had seen the pictures and heard about my interest in becoming a bull-fighter. He said he thought I could go far and offered to sponsor me. He had big plans, said that I should go to a bullfighter school and that until then he would get someone to teach me. He had been to Spain and had long been interested in bullfighting. He said I was just what the *Fiesta* needed—an American girl who could perform well enough to interest Americans—and so on. I was a bit dubious because of the large plans, but I looked him up and could find nothing against him.

He introduced me to an ex-bullfighter he said would teach me for the time being. I was not happy about the teacher. I don't exactly know why, unless that it was his liking for alcohol in too large quantities too often. Anyway, I did not think he was very serious about teaching me. Frank King, who played escort to me for all these meetings didn't seem to be wholly satisfied either, and I was a little worried about it. As I said, I didn't want to make any mistakes in learning. And I knew how very careful of my reputation I would have to be in Latin countries.

One afternoon I met Roberto Monroy, publicity head of the Juárez ring. He too had seen the pictures, and perhaps he sensed that I was not satisfied with my teacher. Monroy promised to help me and said he had a cape I could have. Frank and I went to Monroy's house, where he presented me with my first cape, one which had belonged to the matador Luis Procuna. Then we went back to the ring and he showed me some fancy passes. After each one he'd hand me the cape and tell me to do it.

Later that same week Roberto Monroy called me up at the dormitory. He said he knew of an ex-matador with years of experience who was very good and who might be willing to teach me. He said his name was Alejandro del Hierro, that he had been an excellent matador and was now one of the best *banderilleros* in the business, often acting as the confidential *torero* to leading matadors. He said he was married and had a fine reputation. I made a date to go and meet Alejandro the next day.

I cut geology laboratory and math to keep the date. Frank King took me to the Plaza de Toros in Juárez, where Roberto Monroy introduced me to Alejandro del Hierro. We looked each other up and down; I could see he was trying to be as critical as I was. He was dressed in sweat shirt, khaki pants, and tennis shoes. He was perspiring a little, as he'd been showing a young man how to use the cape when we first saw him.

I asked him all about himself and his experience. I didn't say anything about myself except in answer to his questions. He told me how difficult it would be for me, for anyone. He spoke of fear and how it must never be shown in the ring. He said there was much to learn, that I couldn't hope to perform professionally until after a year or two. I said I wanted to be only a full-fledged matador and not just a novelty. He said, "*Muy bien* [very good]," that he was not interested in a dilettante, and that there was little time for play or social activities in the life of a serious aspirant. I was willing to give up everything, but I wanted to consider it, not let my excitement lead to another mistake. I told him I would consult my sponsor.

"*Muy bien*," said Alejandro again.

Mr. Look took me to the bullfight the following Sunday, and I was able to introduce him to Alejandro. I made up my mind definitely at this time, though I had been certain Alejandro was the teacher I wanted from the first. I told Mr. Look that he was the teacher I wished, rather than the other. I made a date for the following Wednesday for a trial with him; he wanted to see how I handled the cape, how I could run in the ring, and study my coordination. He seemed to think I had possibilities. After watching me do the things he directed, he had me stand against the barrier and count, "one," "two," "three," swinging the cape low in front of me until my arm was flat against the barrier. He ran around the ring, forward and backward with me, following to see how my coordination was. Finally he suggested five exercises for me to do each day at the dormitory.

I could hardly wait to get home to go through the exercises and the one-two-three routine with the cape. I stood in my room with my back against the wall so that I could see myself in the mirror to be sure one hand was not higher than the other. I got up an hour earlier the next morning to go through the routine, and I practiced between classes, hardly able to wait for afternoon so I could get back to the Juárez ring for further guidance. Alejandro was not at the ring when we arrived, but I took my position against the barrier and started the exercise with the cape. Sometime later a man whom I knew to be a picador came by and said, "*Muy bien*," very politely. I had seen this picador in the *corridas* and was pleased that a professional should compliment me, but I was waiting for Alejandro, who I hoped would find me a worthwhile pupil. I asked if he were around, and the picador told me that Alejandro had been stricken with appendicitis.

I was stricken, too! I tried not to show it, and I continued practicing and running. Before I left the ring I went into the chapel again to pray for his health—and my ability to become his pupil, and for success in the art I wished to make my own.

I worked hard every day, both at the ring and at the dormitory. I stopped talking about bullfighting and my ambitions. I didn't mention it in my letters to my parents. I was very serious; no one could even carry my cape for me. I didn't mind the curious when I practiced the running steps around the tennis court at school. I studied before the mirror, and I prayed. This was going to get everything I had, body, mind, and spirit; in fact, I felt it as more spiritual than physical or mental— something that, guided by the spirit, would mold all my faculties into a whole. I remember telling the Virgin one day that the sword would be my life, the cape my *aficion*, and the *muleta* my right arm. Sounds melodramatic, but I meant it. As long as there is a force, an animal to challenge, there must always be a human being to accept the challenge.

It was about two weeks later that I saw Alejandro again—not the straight, lithe man I had met, but one hunched over and walking with a cane. He'd walk slowly around the ring, observing those in whom he was interested. I'd ask how he was when he'd first come by me; at other times I'd ask a question about what I was doing.

He was interested, and I thought he paid more attention to my work than to that of others, but he couldn't show me very well in his condition. I tried to do exactly as he said, and once in a while he'd volunteer a *"muy bien."* This was encouragement supreme, for I was sure that he knew what he was talking about.

One afternoon, when I was practicing after school, Roberto Gonzales, the best-loved impresario Juárez ever had, and Roberto Monroy came by and told me that in a couple of weeks a group of traveling *toreras*—an all-woman *cuadrilla* who always fought together and never with men—would be featured in the ring. They asked me if I would like to do *quites* with them. *Quites* are maneuvers with the cape to take the bull away from horse or man when either are in danger; in this case I knew they meant taking the bull away from the horse and picador after he had been *pic*-ed. In these maneuvers some of the finest work with the cape is possible by an artistic matador. I could hardly believe my ears when they asked me if I would like to try this in an actual *corrida.* I started to blurt out, "Of course!" but then I restrained myself and said they had better ask Alejandro. I kept on practicing, a little leaden in heart, since he had told me before that it would be a year or more before I could appear in a ring in a regular *corrida.* I soon noticed them returning my way, however, with Alejandro. He asked me if I would like to do a *quite* with the women bullfighters. I said I would if he thought it was wise. He said, *"Muy bien,"* and I was in seventh heaven.

Alejandro took me from the barrier and had me combine passes with footwork. He taught me the *gaonera* and the *chicuelina*, two passes that may be used to advantage in *quites*—though I have always started practice with the *veronica*. To this day I am still learning that most basic of all passes, and I'm still not completely happy with the way I do it. The training every afternoon was more interesting as he put me through the steps over and over again. I could hardly sit still in classes, though I didn't cut them. I never went for coffee in between, just practiced. I lived in a world of my own. I had bullfighting shoes made for me. I got a record of *La Virgin de la Macarena* and played it every night before I went to bed. I prayed that I would acquit myself well and that nothing would prevent my going against that bull. Sometimes I could hardly keep from telling an interested friend about it, but I was afraid something might happen. I was sure my parents would forbid it if they found out; as far as they were concerned, I'd forgotten bullfighting.

I tried to get to bed by nine each night. I'd take the cape to bed with me, as a blanket. I'd have the sword and *muleta*, which Francisco Reyes had loaned me, close by. I moved my bed near the window so the moon would shine on it. I'd go to sleep thinking that bullfighting would no longer be just dreaming and hoping, that this was how it would be—doing, not dreaming. At last a real bull. Melodramatic? Perhaps, but very serious to me. I don't laugh at that attitude even now.

But it was not all thrilling anticipation, those two weeks during which I worked under Alejandro's tutelage preparing for my first *quites*. In the first place, Tom telephoned from the East to see why he hadn't been getting letters from me. I should have known better, but I told him, joyfully, that I was on my way to becoming a bull-fighter, that a real teacher was interested, and that I was actually going to do *quites* in the Juárez Plaza de Toros. Well, Tom raved and ranted. Women couldn't and shouldn't try to become bullfighters; it was a man's profession. And on and on. I became furious, too. I don't remember all I said. But I was worried afterward, for he said he would tell my folks. I would have disobeyed them—in this respect, anyway—but I didn't want to worry them. I wanted to prove to them that I could do it, that I had a master, and that I would be taken care of. I felt that if I had been in the ring, and had a competent teacher and setup, they might give their permission. After it appeared in the El Paso papers that I was going to appear in the ring on Sunday, August 12, 1951, I was sure my parents would learn about it and try to stop me. Tom had also said he would come to El Paso and be at the fight.

I was anything but calm and "restful" that Sunday morning as Alejandro had advised. I followed his instructions about eating a late breakfast and, except for that "brunch" at ten, drinking no water. He had said that was important because, if anything happened, blood wouldn't flow as freely as if one drank a lot, and that it kept one in better condition generally. But I couldn't subdue my excitement or stop worrying for fear Tom would show up or something would prevent my doing *quites*.

I was much relieved when Mr. Look came for me at one o'clock and we were on our way. At least there would be no rumpus at the dormitory beforehand. The assistant housemother, Mrs. Crowell, who was staying

63

for the summer session, had been worried enough, but she had been a good sport about it.

I went to the hotel in Juárez where the *toreras* were staying. The matadoras, as the two girls who would kill were called, were Gloria Martinez, "La Gitana," and Teresita Anduluz. I remember trying to talk with them in Spanish and noticing the anxiety that was prevalent. One girl had to leave the room. I felt none of this; there were no butterflies in my stomach then—perhaps because I didn't know enough. I was only conscious of the fact that I would face a real live bull. It was normal enough for them to be tense at this time, however, and they were probably amused at my attitude. I relaxed with them on a bed and tried to talk. They fixed my hair, wetting and oiling it and tying the ribbons I had brought. I wore a man's white shirt and frontier pants with the pockets sewed up, and the *charro* tie that boys who are, or who want to be, bullfighters use for a belt, and a wide cap. I didn't want to emulate an accomplished *torera*, and this seemed the humblest way for me to dress. The girls wore Andalusian suits and hats. They were cute. We walked to the ring—a little late; women!

There was little time to do anything but line up in the *cuadrilla* entrance before the strains of "*La Macarena*" sounded and the gate opened, letting in the brilliant sun. No glitter of *traje de luces*—even the picadors wore the costumes they use on the ranches for testing cows, and Alejandro and the girls' manager, who were to be in the ring in case of emergency, were dressed in *charro* style. But the music of "*La Macarena*" was as though played on my spine; no stage entrance could have been more meaningful for me. I took my place behind the matadoras and felt as though I were floating across the sand to the music and the cheers. I stood behind the *barrera* where Alejandro told me to wait until he signaled to me. There were four bulls, and I was to do *quites* with only one of them.

The first bull entered, the fight progressed, and he was killed. The second went the same way. I began to get anxious. Someone in the seats above yelled, "Where's McCormick?" I had seen friends in the stands who had come to see me. I began to fear I wasn't going to get in the ring with a bull after all.

"*¿Cuando, cuando?*" I called to Alejandro, "When?"

He motioned me to stay where I was. I was about to become an *espontáneo*, and jump in of my own accord to show that I could cape a bull.

The last bull came in. The girls ran him in the preliminary part and the *pics* rode in. I watched Alejandro take the bull away from the horse. He lined him up and yelled for me. I didn't need a second call.

"Get in front of him as though he were someone running with horns in practice," Alejandro said.

I cited him, and he passed beautifully. I turned and flipped the cape over my head to hold it behind me for a *gaonera*. He went by like lightning, and I felt all the confidence in the world as I cited him for another. On the third pass he got me between the legs and I did a double flip, landing plunk on my "caboose." I was mad that the bull had ruined my *quite*. Alejandro and the girls' manager were trying to get me up. I pushed them away, grabbed the cape, and went after the bull. He flipped me again. I got up and tried a *veronica*. He hit me like a freight train and up in the air I went again. I didn't feel any pain; I was just angry. No one could have stopped me then, though I heard the bugles ordering this phase finished and the start of the placing of *banderillas,* and Alejandro yelled for me to leave.

"The bull's been winning over me," I yelled, citing the bull for *chicuelinas.* "I have to win over him before I go!" I passed the bull three times so close he bumped my shins. Alejandro finally grabbed me and dragged me from the ring. But there was applause in spite of my flips, and *Dianas,* that music from the band which is the sign of high approval. I was very happy, though my hair was streaming over my face, and mad that I hadn't got to do a *remate,* where the bull is fixed so you can turn your back to his face and horns and walk away as though Mr. Bull were only a statue.

I stayed behind the barrier until after the kill. Then I enjoyed the congratulations. Someone brought a microphone and I said something—I don't remember what. But I was so happy and radiant I didn't notice that I was sore from all the bumps and tosses. Monroy asked if I would like to kill, and I said, "Sure."

We ran back to the hotel like jack rabbits and changed clothes, still unaware of the bruises. Alejandro was pleased. Mr. Look took me back to the dormitory, and I ate ice cream with Mrs. Crowell, who was relieved to find me in one piece. She told me they had broken up the tea that afternoon early so they could all go and see me in the ring. I told her a little of how I felt, but I wanted to be alone with my joy again.

I went to eight o'clock class the next morning as though nothing had happened, though I was now very conscious of my bruises. I didn't see the papers until later, and I was worried for fear it would all be in the papers my folks would see, but at least it was accomplished and couldn't be taken away from me.

That afternoon, after my last class, I went to Juárez and the Plaza de Toros to continue my practice and to ask Alejandro what I had done wrong.

Four

Flights and Falls

I could overlook my bruises in the knowledge that I had passed a live bull without permitting him to frighten me away from a position I had taken, but there were many things that seemed suddenly to gather their forces to try to dissuade me from what I wanted to do. Perhaps it is better to say what I *had* to do, for after the taste I'd had in the plaza at Juárez, I knew that I would have to go on with bullfighting.

In the first place, because he was present, was Tom. He had not reached me before the fight, but he came to the plaza and argued the next day, and he called that night and threatened again to tell my folks what I had done and how awful it was.

Then there was the fact that the summer session at college was about over and, if I were to stay in El Paso until the fall term opened, I'd have to find some place other than the dormitory in which to live.

Also, the fact that I had a teacher didn't mean that I was launched on a bullfighting career. I would have to get practice with live animals, perhaps on a ranch in Mexico, if that were possible for me, an American girl with little experience. I was willing to leave everything up to Alejandro as far as teaching was concerned, but I couldn't expect him to do more than give instruction and advice.

Most important, of course, was the attitude my parents would have when they learned, as they must, that I had been in the ring with a bull and was determined to continue bullfighting. I knew that they would most certainly disapprove. I had kept it from them because I didn't want to worry them, and I felt that if I had actually tried it, they might be less adamant against my following such a career. Tom's threats and his claim that he had phoned them and told them I had been hurt, I thought, were bluffs so far. But I decided that the only thing for me to do was to telephone Father and Mother and tell them myself. I got Mr. Look to speak to them, too.

I talked with Dad first. He was astounded, to put it mildly, then angry. He said I had disobeyed, and all that. Mr. Look told them I had possibilities, that I had done well for a first time in the ring. He gave them his references and background; he said I had a good teacher in Alejandro, whom he had looked up and found to be good in every respect. He said that I was all right, had not been hurt, and merely wanted their approval to continue. After their first surprise my parents seemed so calm about it all that I was hopeful of their approval which, in any case, I badly wanted.

I sat down and wrote them a long letter after the phone call, expressing my happiness over their calmness and attitude. I felt their attitude took a load off from my shoulders in more ways than one. Of course I loved them and wanted them to approve for that reason alone. Also, I knew that Alejandro probably would not continue teaching me if they told him they did not approve. And the principal weapon Tom was trying to use to prevent me from following my ambition would be removed if they did not object. I tried to make it a joyful letter. I joked about not being disinherited and complimented them on their attitude.

But I was under false assumptions if I thought they had acquiesced so easily. Mother answered my letter at once and said they were coming down the following week end.

"Under no circumstances will you ever be 'disinherited,'" she wrote. ". . . I am devouring your letter trying to find some evidence that you do not intend to consider this idea of becoming a bullfighter—professionally or otherwise. I am a very hurt and confused mother. There are many things I want to say, but dare not lest they be misinterpreted. Our hope is that you will come to see, for yourself, what a grave mistake you are fostering."

She spoke of the pageantry that "had impressed and enthralled" me as a child, and about my being of age and its being my life. "Mr. Look's expression, 'Her very heart and soul are in this thing,' keeps ringing in my ears. You haven't had time enough to place such a burden on your heart and soul. . . . I can take no credit for my mild behavior, I was under a mild case of shock. . . . Most certainly we do not give our consent or permission for you to continue in this field."

She spoke of my education, said that I would certainly not need a degree to fight bulls, and that what I did after I had my degree was, she supposed, out of their hands. "That will be for you to decide." She was hurt that I had devoted so much time to this business rather than to my schoolwork and urged that I could still finish within the year if I concentrated upon my studies. She said they intended to send me back to school only if I promised to work and finish my education before starting anything else.

While she was writing the letter, Mother got one from Tom—"a long letter and a clipping." Mother said she was able to appreciate his letter, "not only because of the interest in your welfare, but because it held our viewpoints on the matter. It was written as one friend would write to another on some serious business and, although it worried me, for some of the contents weren't pleasant to comprehend, it was true, and for that I'm grateful for his friendship. Don't you get 'huffy' about it!" She concluded by saying that she was sick with worry and that she and Dad would be in El Paso to see me the next Sunday. She added a postscript to say that Tom had just phoned and said that I had been hurt in the ring.

I was sunk and, at the same time, angry. I was not hurt, aside from still slightly painful bruises, and I had hoped too much for their approval. I was not angry with Mother and Father, but with my supposed "boy friend." He knew I was not hurt. I considered his telling Mother this a foul blow. I realized, however, that I would gain nothing by not controlling my anger and dismay. I resolved that I would not get excited when my parents arrived, but try to calmly explain that I had to do this thing, however incongruous it seemed to them. As for Tom, I was through with him, whatever he said or did in the future. There wouldn't be time for boy friends for a long time to come anyway, if I seriously devoted all my time to becoming a full-fledged matador.

Alejandro told me one afternoon that I could fight again with the *toreras* on September 9, and this time as a matadora, taking the bull alone for the *faena* (the last act with sword and *muleta*) and the kill. The *toreras* and the impresario had invited me. Of course I accepted, keeping my fingers crossed that my parents wouldn't prevent me. I would have to wait until Sunday to cross that bridge. In the meantime I would add the *muleta* and sword to my practice and try not to worry about problems.

I didn't have long to worry about my parents. They decided not to wait for Sunday to visit me, and took me by surprise. I was reading about Carlos Arruza when Mother charged into my room. The fireworks are on, I thought. Every time I come across Arruza something happens, but it always turns out for the best.

"What happened to you?" Mother cried.

"What do you mean?" I said and jumped up and went to her to show her I was all right.

She looked at me and sort of felt me as though to assure herself that I was whole, and then sat down with a sigh and started scolding me. She said Dad was at the Dean's office checking my grades, and that if they weren't up and I didn't drop bullfighting as a "subject," they'd take me out of school.

I had resolved to be calm, but I never had experienced the calmness I felt. I could understand my mother's feelings in the matter. I realized how much they had done for me and what hopes they had had for a normal life for their only child. I realized how much worry my actions had caused them, and understanding all this I could listen patiently and answer quietly and try to explain as rationally as possible.

"Either you give it up or——" Mother burst into tears.

But she was so relieved that I wasn't hurt, and so surprised at my attitude and lack of excitement—where heretofore I guess I'd argued childishly and impatiently —that she followed her "either or" remark seconds later with what looked like a hopeful sign.

"If I let you do this, I feel I'd be making a great mistake. Someday I'd regret it." She sat looking out of the window at nothing at all, as though trying to divine the future.

I had a pang then and prayed a little that I'd never give them great sorrow or cause for remorse. But Mother hadn't given up. Not that easily! She was going over again all the reasons why a lady did not try to become a bullfighter and about wasted talents, when Dad came into the room. I went to him, trying to smile and show how all right I was. He looked me over a little sheepishly and then looked at Mother.

"Well," he finally said, "She has passing grades."

Then, as though that were too much in favor of the things I'd been doing, he turned to me.

"Seems you've been sneaking behind our backs?" It was more like a question than a statement.

"It's the only way I could do it," I said and looked him straight in the eyes, calmly.

After a little more talk, things quieted down and I said I'd like to have them meet Mr. Look and Alejandro. My Dad said he certainly intended to meet Mr. Look. But I could see that they wouldn't stand in my way if I really wanted to do it. I made arrangements by phone to meet Mr. Look and Alejandro the next day and went off with Mother and Dad to dinner, trying to cheer them up.

Alejandro brought Delia, his wife, to our meeting the next day and she was a big help, being the fine person that she is. Mother and Father also liked Alejandro and Mr. Look, and finally they said I could give bullfighting a trial, at least the fight with the *toreras* on September 9. No, they would not attend it! They wanted to know where I was going to live, since I had to leave the dormitory the following week. Mr. Look assured them that I would be taken care of in that respect, as Alejandro assured them I would be taken care of as much as possible in the ring with the bull.

My parents left on Sunday. Their last words were that they hoped I'd return to school when the fall semester started and finish my college education. I would cross that bridge when I got to it. I had been invited to a hacienda in Aguascalientes by Don Ramiro Gonzales, a good friend of Alejandro. Aguascalientes is the heart of the fighting-bull country, and Alejandro had lived

75

much of his life there. I didn't mention this to Mother and Dad at the time, since my visit would be during schooltime that fall. I felt it more than likely that if I was successful on the ninth of September, and Alejandro would keep me as a pupil, I would not return to school but would devote all of my time to becoming a professional.

I was elated, of course, by the way things were going. It was a relief not to have my family in the dark. I was to have a chance for a complete performance with a good bull, picked for me by Don Ramiro, and I had heard Alejandro's reasons for taking me as a pupil. He told my Dad that I had the head, figure, and valor for a matador. He said I could become a classical fighter with this equipment and much work. He said he would like to prove that a girl could be trained to do all the things a top matador can do—more—not just the specialties so many reputations are now built upon, but everything—the art and the domination. He had emphasized that it would take time. This was great encouragement for me.

I still had other problems, but they seemed minor. I had stayed longer than usual at the dormitory and had a hard time finding another place that would be suitable for a girl alone.

Mr. Look, who had assured my parents I would be taken care of, had left town before I moved out of the dormitory. I wanted to be particularly careful, since I could allow no possible opportunity for gossip about my doings; it was bad enough just to be bullfighting! Mrs. Crowell finally helped me get into a Roman Catholic home for working girls, though I could be promised a room only for two days. I couldn't find a satisfactory place even then, so another girl in the home took me in with her. I lived out of a suitcase, the room was so small. We shared a bath with a spinster who looked askance at me, as did some of the other elderly women. The nuns kept praying that I'd give up bullfighting and were all very good to me. One sister in particular prayed for me and was unusually kind. Most of the nuns were Spanish.

I was very careful. I left the Juárez plaza in time to get home before eight o'clock, but there was still talk by some, though I'm sure it was because they couldn't understand a "nice" girl's wanting to be a bullfighter. I stayed at that home, with that kind girl, until the middle of October. Dad helped me with my expenses, for which I was very grateful, particularly since I knew he didn't approve of what I was doing. He has been very tolerant. Think of all he spent on my schooling, only to have me quit with one semester, or two at most, necessary for a degree!

There was still a little unpleasantness with Tom. I couldn't avoid him when he'd come to the plaza when I was trying to practice, but I refused to go out with him, day or night, after I moved to the Catholic home. There wasn't anything he could do about it except argue in public at the ring, and he soon got tired of that, since I paid little attention to what he said after the first time or two. I concentrated as much as possible on learning to use the *muleta*, that small scarlet cloth used in the last act of the *corrida*, and the sword. Alejandro spent most of his time in the plaza teaching me.

I still went to the little plaza chapel every day, and

after the arrival of the bull I was to fight, I'd go and talk to him. I called him *"mi hijo"* (my son), though his name was—believe it or not—Ferdinando! He was only two and a half years old, what they call a *becerro,* but a very good young animal, the best of the four bulls scheduled for the *corrida.*

I had to wait half an hour for the girls on the ninth, and I was a little impatient. I had a funny feeling that I can't describe. It wasn't exactly anxiety, and it wasn't the carefree excitement I'd had before the *quites.* I got over part of it during the parade into the ring, though I had to wait for the third bull, my Ferdinando. People in the seats above me kept yelling, "When is McCormick coming out?" There were people I knew there and others from across the border who had come to see what an American coed could do.

Finally Ferdinando charged into the ring, with the challenging attitude of a complete conqueror. I did *veronicas* and *gaoneras,* in which the cape is held behind the back, one side extended. The fighter's body is exposed in front of the cape. I was knocked down once, but got *Dianas.* Alejandro said my *chicuelinas* were good.

I was calm when it came time to take the *muleta* and sword and go before the judge to ask permission to kill the bull. Then I went out and cited him for the *pase de la muerte* (the classic pass of death), in which the *muleta* is held in both hands with the sword supporting it and is raised straight up as the horns reach the cloth. It was a terrific thrill to do that the first time and to feel the plunging force rise up after the *muleta* right under my arms. I did it again, and again he charged and surged up into the air trying to catch the lure. The third time he got me. I knew he was going to, but I had made up my mind when I took that *muleta* and sword that I wouldn't step aside once I'd challenged him. I lifted the *muleta* too soon, or too high, or something. My feet were together, but his horn caught me between the legs and lifted me right up onto his back.

I tried to grab his shoulders and push against the horns at the same time. My elbows caught on the *banderillas*. At the same time I tried to figure out what I was going to do when I got off. He got going and I rode him for a while. I heard my shirt tear and the *banderillas* cut me, but I didn't think too much about what mistake I'd made so much as what I'd do next. Then all thought was interrupted as I went *boom* and landed, not very dignified.

I heard a woman yell, "Get that girl out of there!"

Alejandro took the bull away and lined him up again. He told me I should have tried *pases por alto* (high passes), rather than the *muertes*. I cited Ferdinando again and did two *pases por altos*, right-hand passes with the *muleta* held high. Then I put the *muleta* in my left hand, without the sword, and did three low *naturales*. I could hear the crowd and finally the music. It was a wonderful feeling—which didn't last long. On the fourth *natural* I took him too close and he turned too quickly and I got bumped.

I tried *naturales* again and did four in a row, successfully. Then I did a *pase de pecho* with the left hand, bringing the bull from behind up past my chest and

79

under the arm. Then six *redondos de costado,* turning slightly with the bull while doing a low pass, and then *manoletinas,* where the inside edge of the *muleta* is held with left hand behind the back as the cloth is extended high with the right hand, followed by a *remate,* which fixed him. I walked away to the music and cheers and prepared to kill.

One of the girls ran across his line of sight after I lined him up and the bull charged me before I could even make an entrance for the kill. (She had no business even being in the ring at this time.) I was again thrown on top of Mr. Ferdinando, but I slid off quickly this time and lined him up again.

I went in between his horns and felt the sword sink easily into the right place, all the way to the hilt. It was a good kill and the music played again as the people stood and cheered.

I was awarded an ear and made several turns about the ring while hats, flowers, and even money bags showered down from the stands. I carried a bouquet in one arm and held the ear up in the other hand, while Alejandro tossed things back. I put on a sombrero someone sailed down and went to the center of the ring for a last salutation. When I threw the hat back I yelled, *"¡Viva Mexico!"*

I felt no pain whatever. I was exhilarated beyond words. I felt more than ever that I was meant to be a *torera*—yes, even a full-fledged matador. I hurried to the hotel and changed clothes. My roommate and her boy friend took me back to the home. I telephoned my folks and they sounded not only relieved but happy for me. Then I took my roommate and her friend out to dinner in celebration.

I had a hard time going to sleep that night. I was still exhilarated, all worked up. I tried to think what I could have done better and about the mistakes I'd made. And for the first time I knew the feeling of affection for the bull, who is the enemy but upon whom the excellence of the fight depends. Poor Ferdinando had been a brave, if temperamental, bull, doing his best, following the instincts of centuries of breeding, and I had not done him justice. He had deserved a perfect fight.

Don Enrique, brother of Don Ramiro, had Ferdinando's head mounted for me. I still keep it in my room. He's still *"mi hijo."*

I was let down the next day. The bruises were very sore, and the trouble with Tom had gotten me down, and here I was still living out of a suitcase in another girl's room. Though she never said anything, she must have wished for the room to herself again. I didn't want to go to see my folks until I had more definite plans. I knew they would continue to try to talk me out of a bullfighting career.

I went back to practice. I learned what I had done wrong, and what had been good. I was told the papers were full of it, and eventually I looked at the reports with pleasure and some amusement. I continued to practice every day and spent time at night rubbing down the welts on my legs. It was all sweat and grind, without the elation of a fight with a bull or the prospect of a definite fight, but I kept determinedly at it.

Sometimes when the ring was being prepared for a

corrida, or a boxing ring was being erected in it, I'd practice in the *arrastre*, where the dead bulls are taken to be cut up. There were often stench, flies, and filth, but they only reminded me of how far I had to go and how hard I had to work to reach the *cumbre*. If I ever missed a day I lost my peace of mind.

Alejandro found me working in the *arrastre* one afternoon, and during our talk I repeated how I wanted to be more than a *torera*, just a female bullfighter. I wanted to fight with and on an equal basis with men, in the regular category of matador. I didn't want the lesser standards of *toreras*; I didn't want to be a novelty, as a girl or as a North American. I had always had the obsession to fight like a man.

Alejandro told me that in order to accomplish this I would have to be accepted into the union and would have to have a manager. He asked me if I had anyone in mind that might manage me, and start me toward acceptance by the union as a matador *de novillos*, or *novillero*, as a bullfighter is called before being given the *alternativa* by a full matador *de toros* and thereby becoming a full matador himself. In the *alternativa* a full matador hands a *novillero* his sword and *muleta*, permitting the younger to fight and kill his bull during a regular *corrida*. This is the diploma!

I hit the ground again, figuratively speaking, harder than when Ferdinando had tossed me. I knew of no one whom I could ask to manage me. I would have liked Alejandro, of course, but I didn't think he could take the time. I certainly wouldn't ask him, for fear of leaving him out on a limb if something happened.

Then he offered to do it. I couldn't believe it at first; it seemed too much to hope for. I wanted to be sure he wanted to. There was no mention of contracts, but he said that at least he would represent me with the Union of Matadors and Novilleros, as the official association is called.

So I worked harder than ever to deserve him.

Sometime later the *aficionado* club of El Paso presented me with a gold medal. On one side was the image of the Virgin of Guadalupe and on the other was engraved: *La Tauromaquia Society, 9.9.51.*

Alejandro talked to the group about me and the possibilities of a career as a matador. He told them that hereafter, as far as he was concerned, I would fight only with men; that I was going to follow the pattern of the *toreros:* try to become a *novillero,* and ultimately a matador *de toros.* This brought cheers and, of course, made me very, very happy.

There had been no feminine member of the Union of Matadors and Novilleros since Conchita Cintron, the fine *rejoneadora* who fought so beautifully on horseback. She did often kill on foot but was not classed as a matador. I believe that she was the only woman with such category, though years ago there was a Spanish woman bullfighter who followed the rules and standards of the men—Juanita Cruz. She too was good, but she never took the *alternativa* as matador *de toros,* according to Alejandro.

I had been giving the idea of complete dedication to such a career very serious thought, since my parents had given their permission and I had had an experience in the ring with a live bull. I had learned from Alejandro that it would mean the sacrifice of everything most girls hold dear, as well as work and bruises, perhaps the destruction of appearance and feminine attractiveness. I had been trying to consider every disadvantage. I did not in any way wish to go into it as a dilettante or just because of the dreams of a romantic child. I could sum up nothing that outweighed my ambition and the feeling that bullfighting was the thing I had to do. Of course it would be a gamble to go all out, but wasn't that what I'd always wanted? I therefore made my own announcement when my turn came to speak at the *aficionado* club.

"I am dedicating myself to the task of becoming a matador *de toros*," I said, humbly, almost choking. "I am aiming at the highest. I desire the same consideration and chances as are given to the men. I am giving up school and everything else that can in any way interfere with carrying out this idea.

"I have always had the obsession to fight like a man. I considered myself, even as a child, a *torero*, not a *torera*. To have honor in the ring like a matador—the truth, the *pundonor*—that is what I want. That is my ambition and the goal I shall work toward."

So, there it was. I was committed. It was a great relief to me to have made the decision, to know that I had burned the bridge behind me, for there could be no going back for me now. Only inability, a crippling accident, or some force of circumstance beyond my control could prevent me from reaching the peak which had loomed so enticingly since the age of seven. No matter what else happened I could never give up now. My own idea of *pundonor*—that bullfight expression which means more than its definition of a sense of honor, nobility, and integrity—required me to see this through to whatever end.

Five

The Jealous Bulls

If I had thought I was through with school when I decided not to return to Texas Western, I was very wrong. I really had never known schooling until Alejandro took me completely under his tutelage. He had warned me that I would be treated like a man, as far as instruction, practice, and bullfighting went. But that was exactly what I wanted. He told me that, in the school in which he had been trained as a bullfighter, teacher and pupil were in a master-disciple relationship that demanded complete obedience on the part of the pupil, not only in the matters concerning bullfighting, but in every aspect of living.

He wisely did not draw up any contract at this time; he did not wish to be bound to one who could not "take it," and though he seemed confident of my ability to learn and of the other necessary attributes that might make me capable of developing into a good matador, he probably wondered if it would be possible for a girl, raised in the comparatively free atmosphere of North American family and school life, to stick to the almost monastic regime he had known and which he still believes is the only proper way to follow in developing any serious aspirant in bullfighting.

It was no hardship on my part to promise to forego dancing, drinking cocktails, and smoking. Parties seemed very unimportant compared with a career in the Plaza de Toros. I liked dancing well enough, but it was also easy to give it up. Even while still at school I had taken every opportunity to practice and had not minded the fatigue, sweat, and drudgery of repeating the same thing over and over again. But I doubt if even as a child at home I had been so dependent upon permission before doing anything.

"With my master, we didn't even eat without permission." Alejandro said of his teacher.

Alejandro has little use for the dilettante approach. He believes the older schools of bullfighting, which were very exacting and which required long apprenticeship in the *cuadrilla* of a master, were far superior to the rapid rise, and often as rapid decline, that is more usual today with young *toreros*. He believes in the long, slow, sure progress, where every phase of the art is learned.

For ten of the fifteen years that Alejandro del Hierro was a matador *de toros*, he was under the thumb of his maestro and manager, Jose Rodriquez, known in the plazas as "Feria."

Feria had served under an older maestro, who in turn was the disciple of yet a former *torero*. He believed that no one could learn bullfighting as an art and a science without the knowledge that only can be handed down from teacher to pupil, knowledge that never can be formulated exactly enough to write it down. It is an esoteric thing that only can be learned in the relationship of master and disciple—and much of it only intuitively through that relationship. Alejandro too believes this to be the classic method. To the day of Feria's death, Alejandro would behave toward the maestro with veneration and respect.

He tells how Feria once took him to a bar and ordered him to drink a glass of whisky. Alejandro refused, politely, three times, because he had never taken a drink in Feria's presence. Feria became incensed that Alejandro could refuse to obey, and demanded, with some anger, that Alejandro drink. Alejandro drank the whisky. Feria made him consume two more *copas* and then studied him for a while.

"*¡Bueno!*" he said finally, "You can hold it. I had to know, for I am going to die."

Feria died within a month.

The stories about the wild, loose life of bullfighters are not generally true, according to Alejandro. At least not true of the really great matadors who survive long careers.

The tragic death of Manolete in Spain was due more to his infatuation with a girl than to the rivalry and consequent competition of Luis Miguel Dominguin.

Manolete had successfully fought many far more difficult bulls than the one which gored him.

"The bulls are jealous. A matador should be as virginal as the fighting bull fresh from the range. If he is not serious and in good condition, the bull will not respect him, and there will not be a good *lidia*."

Feria was a Spaniard and in bullfighting was of the classical school of his native Seville: both artistic and dominating, with class in all the aspects of the *corrida*. Often a matador is famous for his work with the cape or with the *muleta,* or as a killer; but Alejandro thinks there are few matadors today who dominate all parts with art, though some of the more recently retired matadors came near to his standards.

As a matador, Alejandro fought in plazas with such figures as Armillita, called the "maestro of maestros" because he so well dominated all the *suertes* (acts), but Alejandro says he lacked art, in the sense that another great, Pepe Ortiz, had it. Ortiz, he thinks, was the greatest artist, had the essence of pure art. Lorenza Garza, a strong, dynamic personality, seemed to lack nothing and was particularly a figure with his left-hand passes. Silverio Perez and Juan Silveti, creole types, were gay and dramatic, and the latter's son, Juanito, is a great *torero*, too. Alejandro also highly respects the immortal figure Rodolfo Gaona. Of course Alejandro appeared as matador with many others, but these are the names I heard most when he spoke to me of art, domination, or technique. Since his retirement as a matador, Alejandro has fought with many as *banderillero,* and of these he thinks perhaps Jesús Córdoba (also, by the way, born in the United States) and Juanito Silveti the nearest to classical fighters. He fought that season, the first with me as his pupil, in the *cuadrilla* of Córdoba.

I poured over old copies of bullfight magazines, as I had done at college, only now I could ask about some fighter or some phase of the *corrida* that was mentioned in the magazines and draw out Alejandro. Gradually I realized that one could probably never know everything about the science. My respect for masters, present and of the past, increased—became more truly veneration than the awe in which I had held them as an *aficionado*, before I could appreciate what they really had been.

Being an *aficionado* may be similar to being a fan in the United States, but the feeling of *aficion* to me is an indescribable something that is part religious and part similar to the feeling of patriotism. It involves truth, integrity, and the effort for perfection—not in the sense of order, I guess, since my room always lacks that! It is primarily spiritual, even when its outer form is pageantry and ceremony. Like love and true religion, it defies definition. Carried over into the actual practice and serious desire to be a bullfighter, *aficion* involves discipline, for me—particularly self-discipline—staying at it, trying to reach the stage where every act is intuitive rather than carefully reasoned.

My choice of a career meant the sacrifice of many things women cherish. But I've been feminine from the beginning. I like women to be women and men to be men, even though I am trying to become a matador. I don't want any special favors as a woman, and I would resent any deference on the part of the men *toreros* simply because I happen to be a girl. In some ways I've been more isolated because of my sex, but I believe all matadors are much to themselves, however many friends they may have. There is something in each that can never be shared and which is alone, however many are present. I have tried to keep straight lines and take no feminine advantage in or out of the ring, though I'm not a tomboy. I have to keep my fingernails cut almost to the quick to handle the capes, and the costume I wear in the ring is that of an Andalusian man, the *traje de campero*. But I am feminine.

I have read and heard—chiefly at the early stage— that I never could make a career for myself not only because I was a woman, but because I was not a Latin; that only a Latin possesses the temperament and the understanding of the mystery involved. I do not think it is a question of race or nationality. North American or Spaniard or Mexican, each will fight his own way with his own style. Perhaps Latins are generally less "cold" than more northern peoples; it seems natural that they would understand the *Fiesta Brava* better after centuries of participation in it. They do not see it as a cruel thing, which it is not, and they get spiritual satisfaction from the art and nobility with which a man, like themselves, puts aside his fear to accept the challenge of brute force and vicariously offers himself to show that forces can be met and overcome by courage and faith and skill.

A North American with integrity, who gets spiritual satisfaction from answering a challenge nobly, can also be good in the bullring.

Harper B. Lee, the first North American professional bullfighter, was very well spoken of in Spanish countries. Sidney Franklin, the Brooklyn boy who went to Mexico and then to Spain, where he lives today on a bull ranch, won the plaudits of Latins everywhere. So I am not the first North American bullfighter. I was actually surprised to learn that I am the first North American woman professional fighter. I haven't tried to change my temperament. I refused to change my Scotch-Irish name. If these are handicaps, I'll overcome them, with harder work and greater application. Certainly a boy raised on a bull-breeding ranch or in the tradition of a bullfight family has advantages over those who have not shared these inborn or early environmental advantages, but there have been *toreros* who reached the top without them.

Alejandro did treat me as he would have treated a boy; he could be sharp when I was slow to learn, and there was little sympathy with failures or careless work. Practice became more strict. Any fat I had was soon lost in the practice, either by myself with the cape, or with someone running with the horns to simulate a bull, or with the cart, like a wheelbarrow with horns built up on it, that Alejandro or someone else would rush at my *muleta*, guiding it as though it were a bull with eyes for the best target presented. If I exposed myself, the cart hit me as a bull would. I did not mind. I was doing what I had wanted to do, and if there was no glamour in the routine and work, the knowledge that I was learning under a good teacher kept my dedication unwavering.

Aside from this, there were the prospects of going into the heart of the bull country in Aguascalientes to work out against live animals. That these would be mostly cows being tested for fitness to mother brave bulls did not lessen my anticipation for the venture. I had heard about *tientas*, as the testings are called, and about the

93

great haciendas where they are held. Glamorous Mexico may have lost its gypsy romance for me with the years, but not its romance. I was eager for it and prayed that it would soon come about that we could go deep into Mexico and visit these ranches, see the bulls on the ranges, test the cows, and live the life.

After his first mention of it, Alejandro talked little about my visiting there. Once he told me that it had been postponed, but he said no more about it before telling me to get ready. I was eager to leave the home where I was crowding my kind roommate almost as much as I was anxious to get into Mexico farther than just across the Border.

Mother and Dad visited me again after my first kill. They were not exactly happy about me, but, having given permission for me to try it out, they were lending their moral support. I think they hoped to find that I was weakening in my desire to be a bullfighter, but they became reconciled to the fact that I was more determined than ever.

"You'll have to mature very rapidly," my dad said. "You'll have to develop judgment. The real test will be yourself."

There were amusing aspects, too, aside from family emotions, hard work, and the pleasures of anticipation. Newspapers printed stories about me that were not always as accurate as they were sensational. I was called "the blonde Goddess of the Bullring" until I worried lest the appellation stick. None of the articles took me very seriously, though there were critics who, admitting my lack of knowledge, said I had much promise. Mary Thurber, the bullfight critic of the El Paso *Times* had written of my first kill: "When she is working coolly and not in trouble, she gets the feeling of art that all great *toreros* have. Some call it emotion. At any rate, she's got it." To most of the other writers north of the Border, I was a novelty or a freak working in a field they did not understand.

I had a proposition from a national carnival outfit, who offered to put me on their circuit. They didn't care how I faked it; they would bill me as a matadora and pay well. Agents wanted to sign me up for possible motion-picture work. There was an editorial by a nationally known commentator inveighing against me and my parents for embarking on such a barbarous and inhumane career.

The only proposition which we considered seriously at this time was an offer to simulate a fight, with live bulls, in Chicago. Alejandro found that he couldn't take fighting bulls across the Border, and we went out onto the Texas range and tried caping Brahman bulls; but their characteristics were so different from those of bulls bred for the ring that we gave up the idea. Those Brahmans wouldn't carry a charge through even on the range. They'd stop short of the cape. When they hit, however, they hit as hard as any other bull—like a freight train!

I was practicing in the Juárez ring when Alejandro came and told me to pack and get ready to leave for Aguascalientes. I didn't need any urging. I moved all my things which wouldn't be necessary to Delia del Hierro's mother's house in El Paso, and with two suitcases I boarded the Aguascalientes bus with Alejandro. At last I was going deep into Mexico for the first time since I was seven. And with a real *torero* for escort!

It was romantic, all right, that long journey halfway down the length of Mexico (with a brief respite in Chihuahua), on through the mountains to Durango, Zacatecas, and finally to the city of Aguascalientes on the central plateau of Mexico, six thousand feet above sea level. I don't know why I was surprised to find the city so large—it has a population of almost one hundred thousand—but I had heard of and enjoyed seeing its old cathedral and fine old houses. Many of the streets that now are paved were torn up that first time I was there, but just going around them and seeing the old colonial mansions were romantic for me. Many of them surpassed my childhood ideas of palaces, and I could not help thinking about the city's long history, from Spanish colonial days through the struggles for independence, the reign of Maximillian and the tragic Carlotta, and more recent revolutions. In the central plaza they still have promenades on Thursday nights, as in the days of the conquest.

But my maestro was anything but romantic. He thought that I talked too much and asked too many questions about things that did not pertain to bullfighting, and he made it plain that this was no pleasure trip, but one solely for business, to give me a chance to work with live animals.

However, I was introduced to his friends, the Dr. Oscar Hernandez Duque family, and they all became my friends—such friends, in these short years, as one rarely knows. The lovely Señora, Chebela, has been more than gracious, as we shall learn later, as has the doctor's sister, Socorro. I met her daughter Marta later in San Luis. Her too I prize as a real friend. The doctor's house and offices are beautiful and built around a fountained courtyard. We spent much of our time at that house the first visit, and every time since, when we have been in Aguascalientes. I love those people.

We found that Don Ramiro's cows had already been tested in regular *tienta*, but he let me retest some. Cows learn much faster than the bulls, and with their previous experience they were difficult. They turned on me faster and kept changing their form of fighting so that it was hard to figure out what they would do next.

We fought them in a stone corral, rather than in the miniature ring generally used for *tientas*. Once I was in the enclosure, there was no place to escape, unless it was scrambling over the wall where it was going to pieces. I wore a shirt and blue jeans, and Spanish boots loaned to me by Dr. Duque.

I learned first hand some of the truth of what is said about the female of the species; it certainly comes out in a cow! Alejandro had to work them down until they would charge the cape, and then I would take them. I fought six of the imps of Satan that day. One young cow gave me my first *puntazo* (slight horn wound). Only Alejandro and Don Ramiro Gonzales were present besides myself. They seemed to think that I did all right under the circumstances. We went to dinner at the Gonzales home in the city, since the family were not living at the ranch. It was a grand day for me.

Aguascalientes is full of bullfighters, ranchers, and others associated with the *corrida*. One of the most picturesque is Señor Garabato, at whose hacienda one of the principal *tientas* is held. A big man, always dressed in *charro* costume and with wide sombrero, one can hear him coming by the clink and jingle of his spurs in the street. I was invited to test at his ranch also, and hoped to do better, since three matadors would be present at his *tienta*—Alfonso Ramirez, Calisero; Luis Castro, El Soldado; and Pepe Luis Vasquez.

They even let me fight a bull at Garabato's, a bull which would be used for breeding purposes, since a fighting bull must never have been fought completely before his appearance in the ring. I can't say I fought this animal (in all phases but the actual killing) perfectly, but I fought well enough so that Calisero and El Soldado recommended, and later vouched for, me to the Union of Matadors and Novilleros as a *novillero*. As though it were not exciting enough just to be in the same *tienta* with such famous matadors!

Alejandro was scheduled to fight in Mexico City, and he took me along so that we could see about getting into the union and obtaining a passport for me, so that I could fight professionally in Mexico. Of course, hoping to get into the Union of Matadors and Novilleros, and thereby becoming a real, authentic professional bullfighter, was most exciting. Nothing less could have topped the thrill of going to Mexico City again, where I had seen my first bullfight, which started all this.

I did get into the union as a *Matadora de Novillos* (first woman since Conchita Cintron) and I did see some of the sights—the plazas, churches, and parks. In the new ring I also saw bullfights with such matadors as the Spanish Martorel and Manolo Gonzalez; the great Mexicans, Silverio Perez and Fermin Rivera; and the North American of Mexican ancestry, Jesús Córdoba, with whom Alejandro fought as a *banderillero*. But I also learned what it is like to be a professional *novillera* under the tutelage of a strict maestro. After *"buenos dias"* in the morning, almost everything I said was "talking too much." Nothing was ever repeated to me after the first time; if I didn't get it then, I never could hope to. I could not leave my hotel room alone without permission, and it took a good reason to get that permission.

I waited in my room each morning for Alejandro's knock on the wall, the signal that he was about ready to go to breakfast. I was usually ready and waiting and hungry. I would go into the patio to wait for him. Once, while waiting, I was thinking of Luís Freg, the great killer who had been gored scores of times and who died of drowning, trying to rescue children. I decided to ask about him. But Alejandro was abrupt.

"Did you ever fight with him?" I asked.

"I fought with him."

"Was he as great as they say?"

"Yes."

"Was he better than you?" I hoped to draw out more information.

"Of course," in Alejandro's most sarcastic tone, "Why ask such a stupid question? He was more serious than I."

I was learning what the strict classical school was like, and if the charges that all I was after was glamour had any foundation in fact, I would have given up the first month I was with Alejandro.

But I also remembered the responsibility that was his. People had said he was crazy to take me; that he was wrong to allow me to make those *quites* and insane to let me fight and kill Ferdinando; that if I were in-jured or killed it would be all his fault. He was also doing all he could to have me taken seriously in Mexico, as well as to try to train me to become a good matador. He has often told me that the hardest part of a bull-fighter's career is outside the ring, and he takes care of all of that. The more responsibilities and business piled up, the more irritable he became. In addition to this, people were curious about us. I had to learn to be quiet, not to spoil everything. I had to respect his principles, which are of the highest, in bullfighting and out of the ring. I had to justify his faith in me, for his faith alone gave me confidence.

I knew that I was lucky, that probably no other good bullfighter would have given me the chance he was giving me of achieving my one ambition. And so I learned to be disciplined in every respect, as much as any Latin woman could be, and I kept my place. I still look up to Alejandro with reverence and respect, even though my training under him has meant the sacrifice of some of my native North American heritage of inde-pendence. However critical, he has never been degrad-ing; he has never said that I wasn't worth two cents. And he has never lost confidence in me. I asked to be treated as a man pupil, and if he does not think of me as a woman, that is what I want. He always said that compassion toward a pupil does not pay.

Of course a woman is always pleased to be fitted for new clothes—and I was, while in Mexico City. They were not what a lady usually gets, however. They were high-waisted Andalusian pants and a tailored, short, open jacket. I got a wide-brimmed Córdoban hat and a white shirt with frilled front to complete the outfit. This was what I would wear as a *novillero* (professional matador of *novillos*, as bulls under four years of age are called). I was more thrilled than if it had been my wedding gown.

We returned to Aguascalientes for more practice with live animals and then went back to Mexico City to sign contracts with the union and my contract with Alejandro as teacher and manager. It was arranged that my professional debut as a *novillera* would be on January 20, 1952, in Juárez. Then I returned to Juárez alone by bus. Alejandro had been double-crossed by someone to whom he had loaned money, and he had to wait in Mexico City. He fought there twice before returning to Juárez.

I had to borrow money (by writing a check on Dad's account) to get a train ticket home to Big Spring for Christmas. I had much to tell them, and tried to show them how much it meant to me. They seemed resigned to the fate of their child, and they at least pretended to be happy for me.

I stayed home for the Christmas holidays and the New Year, but I practiced every day as well as I could without the advice of my maestro. I kept in touch with him all the time and wondered about the coming debut: what kind of bulls I'd have and who else would be on the program. I knew that they would be men and that the *corrida* would be conducted along the same lines as though I too were a man. I have never fought with women or under other than the union rules since my first kill.

I ate too much at home and started to gain a little

weight. Of course there were dinners and even a New Year's Eve party, which should, perhaps, have been taboo. I practiced in my new Andalusian pants and Spanish boots to get used to the tightness of the uniform, which I noticed was even tighter than the last time I had tried it on at the tailor's in Mexico City. I had to diet.

While I was at home, I made my first appearance on a radio program broadcasted from a studio. This was a benefit for Boys' Ranch of West Texas. The producer, who was also a talent agent, tried to talk me into television appearances in both Hollywood and New York. I demurred but finally agreed to discuss it with Alejandro. After I'd made the radio appearance, the agent said he had been in touch with Hollywood and that there had been many requests on Art Baker's *You Asked for It* for the appearance of a bullfighter and that they wanted me on the show. I telephoned Alejandro, since the agent said Art Baker had to know at once. He added that there were shows in New York that wanted me, too. I finally told him to go ahead and arrange for the Hollywood show and we'd see about New York later, but that I was afraid such shows would interfere with my career as a matador. He agreed that they could be arranged for times after my debut and during February and March, when it is windy all over Mexico and consequently not right for bullfighting.

Mother went with me when I returned to Juárez two weeks before the debut. We stayed at the San Antonio Hotel. I had to remain in Mexico in order to fight there on my artist's passport, but a proper place for a single woman was hard to find. It was quite different being a *torera* wanting to make her career in Mexico than it would have been for a career girl in the United States.

I started intense practice under Alejandro's guidance every day, in either a sweat shirt and blue jeans or my new *traje corto*. First came the cape work, starting always with *veronicas* and then other *lances*, as the cape passes are often called. Then practice with the *muleta* and the sword, and finally the cart with horns to practice the kill.

Mother and I ate at the hotel. We very rarely went to a movie. Dad wrote that we were to appear on ABC television and Art Baker's *You Asked for It* the week end following my debut and that he would drive us all, Mother and Alejandro and me, to California as soon as we could leave after the fight. We finally persuaded him to come to Juárez for my first professional fight, though he thought up a lot of excuses. Mother had agreed to attend, and I reserved front-row seats for them. I think she got almost as much kick out of the posters announcing my fight as I did, but neither she nor Dad were too sure they wanted to see the fight itself.

One morning, when I went to the plaza for practice, they told me that the bulls had arrived. I went to the peepholes where the bulls may be seen in their high-walled corral without disturbing them. I fell in love with the largest, a four-year-old black and white bull, which reminded me of the painting of El Gallo fighting such a bull that had impressed me so when I was very young. I told Alejandro that I wanted to fight that bull, that I felt he would give a good account of himself and make my debut a success.

Alejandro told me to give a good account of myself

with whichever bulls I drew. There were to be two *novilleros* on the program with me. I was to fight two bulls, and they would have one each. I looked at that black and white bull every day after practice. Of course I studied the others a little, too, for I didn't know which bulls would fall to my lot. I didn't have a worry about their size or their horns. It didn't occur to me, during those days of practice, that I could be hurt. I prayed only for fast-charging, brave animals which would give me a brilliant performance—and that Mr. Black and White would be one of them.

Six

Debutante

I have mentioned something about the solitary status of a matador, whether a man or a woman. One of the best examples of this that I can think of is the situation that always prevails when he is to fight. A bull-fight is always a *fiesta*; *La Fiesta Brava* is the most extravagant term for a *corrida*, the unique festival of people of Spanish heritage. The whole town or city takes on a gala mood the day before, a festive spirit that lasts through the night and even through the day after the fight. But the matador, who with the bulls is responsible for all this festivity, takes no part in the celebration before he enters the ring. It is hard for him not to be very conscious of what is taking place around him, however alone he is. Friends may come to his room and wish him well; he may even walk out among the happy crowds on the afternoon or evening before his fight, but he is not one of the celebrants. He is alone with his thoughts; he tries to rest and keep his mind calm and at ease, without too much thought about the ritual he is to perform when the celebration reaches its climax.

Of course I was elated as the week end of my debut arrived; I was the principal reason for this particular fiesta. Not only were many people from El Paso to join the Juárez citizens in the plaza the next day to see what the North American girl could do, but almost fifty people had come from my home town for the occasion. But it was not only my elation that kept me from the prescribed rest. I went to bed early enough, but the celebrating could not be shut out any more than I could turn off my own thoughts.

The San Antonio Hotel is built around a court which rises, balconied floor by balconied floor, to a roof garden. It was in this garden, with its bar, that much of the celebrating by those from across the Border was being carried on. I might almost as well have been up there myself! The melodies of the Mexican orchestra, and the accents of Texans, punctuated now and then by a rebel yell, however enjoyable and at times amusing, were hardly a lullaby. I didn't sleep until the small hours of the morning. I am sure my mother didn't sleep much either, though she made a good pretense of it. She too had her thoughts.

When I woke up—not very late in the morning—it was strangely quiet, but I heard something. I listened, trying to figure out in my half-awakened state what it was that so accented the quiet. It couldn't be a clock, that regular beat? Not rain! I jumped out of bed and pulled aside the curtains. It was raining! I must confess that there was an instant in which I felt relief, relief that the tension was over if I could not fight that day. But it was exceedingly brief. I wanted to fight, and fight well, in a sunny plaza under perfect conditions. I was really sunk, even before the second of relief had time to rise to consciousness.

"It's raining!" I said to Mother, almost ready for tears.

"Really?" she sounded most cheerful. "Then let's have breakfast."

Alejandro came in the early afternoon and said that the fight was scheduled to go on, that the rain had been little more than a drizzle, and that I should proceed on the assumption that I would fight. The doubt in my own mind that there would be a *corrida* kept other doubts from forming in any formidable manner, for the drizzle kept up.

The most cheerful note, up to this point was Alejandro's statement that I would get the best bull, the black and white! But worry about how we would perform in the rain dampened even that joy somewhat.

Big Spring people came to our room for brief visits and to wish me luck. I think, though, it was more to sympathize with Mother than to encourage me, though of course they wished me luck, too. Mother stayed with me while I dressed in the *traje corto*. I left for the ring before my folks did.

It was still raining when the *cuadrilla* gates opened

and I lined up between the other two *novilleros* for the parade into the ring. I felt the lack of sun a bad omen, but I observed that the stands were full. As we crossed the wet sand toward the judge's box to make our bows, I noticed that someone other than Father was sitting next to Mother, but there was no time then to make queries. I had the first bull, and after a smile of confidence at Mother I went right to the opening in the barrier, behind the protecting *burladero* to await him.

The bull was slow to come out, but when he did he pranced, skidded, and fell. When he got up from the sand, he limped. "Holy Virgin," I prayed with all my heart and soul, "don't let this be a fiasco!"

It was obvious that the bull had hurt himself. He could not, or would not, charge the capes well. It looked as though my first bullfight as a professional would be against a nearly helpless cripple. But the bull could be more dangerous to kill if I had to go after him in his chosen terrain, rather than get him to charge me as I directed with the *muleta*. The audience at a bullfight, however, does not realize that a bad or cowardly bull who refuses to charge can be more dangerous than a brave one who tries to carry the fight. It is like trying to fight a defensive boxer who always waits for his opponent to bring the fight to him. A waiting bull just defends himself by hooking, and there are few who can plant the sword properly with such an animal. Because the sympathy of the crowd, who did not understand this, would be entirely with this animal, I took a bold step without asking permission of my maestro. I went to the front of the judge's box and requested permission to waive the picadors—always the most unpopular part of a *corrida* with the fans, particularly with North Americans who do not comprehend the function of the *pics*. The judge granted the request, the picadors were sent from the ring, and the *banderillas* were placed—not too gracefully—on the lame bull.

"You'll never get his head low enough to go in for the kill," Alejandro said sharply in comment on my dismissal of the picadors. But I thought that he approved of my action.

I hate to dedicate a bull I am sure is not going to put up a good fight, but since this was my first as a professional I had resolved to dedicate him to the audience, which I did. There was little I could do with the bull. Perhaps a great matador, with the knowledge of bulls which comes from years in the ring, could have made him fight. I tried to get him to charge, but I was not skilled enough to handle him well. He was interested only in defending himself where he stood. I decided that the sooner I killed him, this dull afternoon, the better. Alejandro, of course, had been right. His hind quarters might be weak, but his neck muscles were in good shape and his head high. Three times he caught me, cradled me between his horns as I went in to kill, and bumped me away from him. This was better than getting a horn hooked into me, but it was quite like a battering ram on my chest and stomach. I finally got the sword in, but he was slow in falling and I had to *descabellar* him, the *coup de grace* which quickly severs the spinal cord just behind the horns. I didn't do it that easily, however, for he still kept hooking upward, and I had to try three times before the life went out of him. It was not pretty.

I walked back to my place, sad and angry. What a

debut. I knew that all the doubters would be quick to say, "I told you so." I knew that few in the audience had enough knowledge to realize that I had been pretty helpless against the circumstances. The leaden sky and the drizzle matched my mood. Mother tried to smile reassuringly when I looked at her. I was glad I couldn't see Dad, whom Mother tried to point out across the ring in the high seats on the other side. He had preferred greater distance from the spectacle, and, I suspect, to avoid showing his anxiety at close range to Mother.

Just then the rain came down in torrents, a fitting pall for the occasion. The crowds streamed out of the stands as quickly.

The second fight with one of the other *novilleros* was not much better, though the bull was uninjured. The *novillero* seemed very nervous and did little that was distinguished until he killed with one good thrust. This was the first thing the crowd could cheer about, and he got a tour of the ring for his feat. The crowd was mostly back in the stands again.

Just as the bugle sounded for the third bull of the afternoon (and my second), the skies cleared and the sun came out brilliantly. It was like a miracle to me. I have always been susceptible to light and shade, and I felt it a grand omen, as the rain had seemed ominous. I turned toward Mother and she leaned down, extending her hand in best wishes.

The black and white tore into the ring and stopped, head high, king of all he surveyed. He charged the vanishing capes of the *banderilleros* and tried to get at the men behind the *burladeros*. Alejandro ran him across the ring, his cape trailing and zigzagging to see how he hooked. I could see that he was frank and quick.

I went out and cited him with confidence. The *veronicas* went off well. I passed him inches away from me and had no trouble until the *chicuelina*, on which he turned most quickly and almost got me. I knew I would have to respect this noble bull. The *quite*, after the *pics*, proved this; he was a fighter and one who learned quickly. Doing a *quite*, I heard women scream as he brushed me close enough to make my clothes bloody.

"Oh, if you could only cook!" a man shouted.

"Get that girl out of there," some woman kept yelling, but she was drowned out in the *Dianas* and applause. I knew that I had a good bull and that I would do everything in my power to give him a good fight. I had lost all doubts about the outcome, though Alejandro was not so sure and plainly told me.

After asking permission to kill, I walked over in front of Mother. Extending my hat up toward her I dedicated this noble bull to her.

"It goes for thee, Mother. I hope this one may be better."

"I have all the confidence in the world in you." Mother said, leaning down and extending her hand.

He was perfect, bless him. I planted my feet and gave him all the *muleta* passes in my repertoire. I never moved while he charged or passed me. Not once did I have to chase him. I would cite and call out endearingly, for I loved the brave bull, and he'd come, close and fast. His horn once ripped my shirt as he tried hooking on the way by. I hated to stop the *muleta* work, but he was learning so fast that if I kept it up he'd know enough to escape the *muleta* and take me. Also he was tiring me. I lined him up and killed him to the bedlam of a screaming, shouting audience. I couldn't tell whether the *"oles"* of the Mexicans were louder than the cheers and yells of those from the other side of the frontier. I went to the dead bull, who had given me such a chance to prove myself and who was responsible for the good performance, and gave him a few pats on the head. I stroked his nose. Then I went to the barrier to bow to the judge.

The crowd still shouted. The judge held up two fingers and Alejandro brought me the coveted ears. I toured the ring again and again, very happy. I located Dad way up in the stands on the sunny side and waved to him. It had been a good debut after all.

"Did I fight like a man?" I asked Alejandro when we were behind the barrier again.

"Sí," he answered. "Yes." But his smile said much more. I knew he was pleased in spite of his worry during the fight. It had been a great responsibility for him.

I stayed through the last fight. The second man did well with his *veronicas* but little thereafter to win acclaim. I could honestly feel that I had performed better than either of the other *novilleros*, while admitting that I had had the best (and the worst) bull. I was surrounded when I tried to leave. I said something into a radio microphone. I signed autographs until my hand was limp. I had to be pushed into the car.

Back at the hotel I embraced Mother and Dad and asked them how they liked it. We were all too emotional to say much that was coherent. People burst into the room, saying they had come from far parts of Texas and couldn't leave without seeing me or getting my autograph. When the reporters came I really felt like a celebrity, but I was most curious to hear what Mother and Dad said when they were questioned.

Mother told a reporter, "I am relieved, proud, and weak. I was afraid and nervous. But if she had the courage to fight those bulls, I felt I should be brave enough to watch it."

"It was hard for me to take it," Father said. "Hard for me to realize that my only child was facing that bull. She has always been fascinated by it, since she was a child visiting Mexico City. I tried to talk her out of it. But she is twenty-one and has made up her mind. She is sincerely serious, and my wife and I will back her up now."

Asked what he thought of his daughter's becoming a celebrity, Father said, "We're trying to be careful about that. The sharks in that line worry me, but not Pat. All she has ever wanted to do is fight bulls. Her head will not be turned by publicity."

I could have gone over and kissed him, but I was pretending to listen to a conversation. Of course one of the biggest thrills was when Alejandro came in and a reporter asked him what my chances were now.

"About three out of fifty make it," he said in Spanish. "Pat is the best of the three. She will go far. You could see how far she outshone the other two this afternoon."

Ah! If all moments were as blissful!

A couple of days after the fight, we left Juárez for California in Dad's car. I would have been happier if we had been leaving for another *corrida* somewhere, but Alejandro wanted me to practice more before fighting again, and besides, there was the wind, the *torero's* worst enemy. We had our equipment, including the practice cart with horns for the TV show, and our bullfighting clothes. In Hollywood we went to the hotel where the agent had told Dad he had made reservations for us. The hotel was full, and no one there had ever heard of us or the agent.

Dad got in touch with the television people at the American Broadcasting Company. They too were wondering about the whereabouts of the agent, but our appearances were scheduled and they made arrangements with another hotel that could take us. I enjoyed doing the shows. Art Baker was very kind, and everyone seemed interested in what we were trying to do. None of them had ever seen a bullfight. I dressed in my *traje corto* for *You Asked for It* and did *veronicas* and a few other passes. We demonstrated the kill with the cart, Alejandro pushing it. Everyone was fine to work with. I almost made myself sick on green apples from an apple machine in the studio. I love them, and they reminded me of times when as kids we'd steal them.

Someone wanted me to take a screen test, but I told them I was just embarking on one career and couldn't even think of trying for another. I did model some clothes for some woman's magazine, and I modeled my costume with a beautiful Palomino horse.

Dad, of course, spent most of his time making inquiries about the missing agent. The latter had complained of heart trouble when Dad had last seen him, so Dad was a little worried, as well as angry that he might have been "taken." We later learned that the agent had left Big Spring with half the money that had been raised for the benefit of the boys' ranch!

We were back in Juárez the fifth of February, Mother and I at the hotel again. Father returned to Big Spring. Alejandro and Delia rented a new house on the outskirts of Juárez that was large enough to include me besides them and their two children. I moved in with them so that Mother could return home. Intensive training commenced again. Alejandro decided to let me fight the end of March in Nuevo Laredo, if I worked hard.

In the del Hierro household we lived, ate, and slept bullfighting. At last I was submerged in the world of *tauromaquia,* the elegant name for all that pertains to bullfighting. There might be a lively discussion at breakfast about some matador or a recent *corrida.* Then off to the plaza for at least two hours' practice in the sun, with the maestro goading or encouraging his pupil. Three o'clock dinner, after a shower and short rest for me, with more discussion, usually about my work. Alejandro often took pictures of our practice, and these might be studied. Sometimes I was happy for praise or commendation, now and then silenced for my ignorance. There might be more practice in the court by the house—with the mounted horns, or just plain practice. Perhaps a walk in the cool of the evening with Martín, Alejandro's brother and my sword handler, and supper around nine at night. Nothing was allowed me that did not pertain to the fighting of bulls. Alejandro didn't like to have me read books, though I could study the bullfight journals. In short, there was but one focus, and almost everything not absolutely necessary was taboo.

The second professional fight, at Nuevo Laredo, was important in being the first appearance away from my home base. Here I was a stranger, known only by the

115

somewhat doubtful publicity engendered by the *quite*, first kill, and debut. I was excited, feeling my wings, until I saw the bulls. Two and a half to three year olds, they seemed small after Mr. Black and White. I had wanted to prove myself with big bulls. I saw these the day before the fight, after we arrived in Nuevo Laredo, and the wind went out of my sails. Alejandro said they looked fast and that a small bull could give as much and often more difficulty than a giant.

Both bulls caught me during the fight. I had a "grayout" when the first threw me against the barrier, but a TV cameraman said I was up in three seconds. I was able to use many *naturales* and made good kills with each of my bulls. The judges gave me both ears and the tail of each. This helped in establishing me in Mexico. Mexican critics have been much more kind to me than most newsmen of my own country and, since they know more about the art, what they say is more important.

In Juárez I fought again in a month. The bulls had been overturned in the truck bringing them up from Aguascalientes. They were so nervous, banged up, and haggard that for a while we didn't think they would be fit for the ring. To quiet them, we had to keep them away from the public for two days. But they fought. I cut one ear.

I fought for five successive Sundays after that, all along the Border, from a repeat fight in Nuevo Laredo in the east to Nogales, just south of Tucson, Arizona. In Nuevo Laredo I was cut under the eye by the first bull and had to make a trip to the infirmary (my first), after I had killed him. Alejandro harangued me all the way there. He said it was my fault, that I hadn't used the

At right: Alejandro del Hierro, teacher and manager of Patricia McCormick, leaning against a *bur-ladero* in the Tijuana bull ring.

Below: Patricia McCormick executes a *pase derechazo* during her debut as *matadora de novillos,* or *novillera.*

Patricia displays the two ears awarded her at her debut in the
Juarez ring. Note the miniature El Paso deputy sheriff's badge,
which was presented to her just before her debut.

At the *tienta* of Pepe Or-
iz, Patricia McCormick
executes the following
passes:

Derechazo

Veronica

Arruzina
(a pass named after the
great matador Carlos Ar-
ruza)

Natural

At left: Patricia McCormic[k] waiting in the *callejón*, betwee[n] bulls, in Nuevo Laredo bu[ll] ring. Notice the cut under h[er] eye from the first bull. Behi[nd] her, Del Hierro is adjusting [the] *palillo* in the *muleta*.

At right: Desplante con adorn[o]. *Desplante* means showing o[ff] and an *adorno* is a fancy pa[ss] or an addition of some sort [to] a maneuver. This was the fir[st] time that Patricia McCormi[ck] handled the bull's horns.

Below: Veronica.

Below: *Derechazo.*

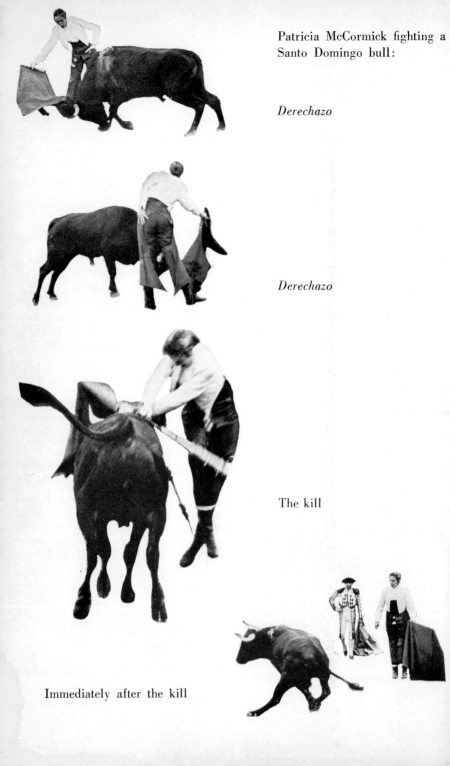

Patricia McCormick fighting a Santo Domingo bull:

Derechazo

Derechazo

The kill

Immediately after the kill

muleta correctly, that I had not killed well. (I'd had an ovation.) I had to return to the infirmary after the *quites* on the second bull to try to stop the bleeding while the *banderillas* were placed. Even during the *faena*, Alejandro was bawling me out, so that when I lined the bull up for the kill, I felt I had the devil behind and the devil in front. I was mad and exasperated. The sword went in easily to the hilt, in the proper place. I didn't notice anything except that the bull was still standing, so I walked over toward the barrier for another sword. When I turned I saw his knees buckle. He was dead. I got two ears and his tail as the crowd yelled. All the time I was touring the ring, Alejandro, following me as he was supposed to and tossing things back that were showered down, kept saying that I didn't deserve ears, let alone the tail. He thought better of it later, but I was sullen up to the next fight at Villa Acuña.

Because of the long journeys (we returned to Juárez after each *corrida*) I was tired, though after the first long bus trip to Nuevo Laredo my Dad had loaned us a car so that Alejandro and the sword handler and I drove by ourselves. I didn't feel well at Villa Acuña; I was leaden in the heat. That was the only fight of my first year when I didn't cut an ear or more. I did get something, however; I dedicated one of the bulls to Don Jesús Ramón, the impresario, and after the fight he took the watch from his wrist and handed it down to me.

"Keep that constantly with you," remarked Alejandro, "to remind you how badly you fought."

That burned like something molten all the way down my gullet, where it stuck like lead. I'd rather have fought well or been gored than to have such judgment from him, whom I was trying to please and whose theories I was trying to prove.

But I was learning, little by little. I discovered what I'd been told—that formulas had to be made to fit each bull as he is fought. I had to learn about terrain and the lines of fight and whether or not high or low passes were best in each situation; to fight as the bull wished until I had him under control so that I could lead him.

The whole summer was one constant effort to find good form for *veronicas* (I'm still learning that) and learning to kill. Killing wasn't difficult for me in the first place. I like it, feel most relaxed and confident in killing, but I still have much to learn in that, too.

Left-hand passes, *naturales*, were the easiest for me. I'd been left-handed as a child until I was made to change. They are the most difficult passes as a rule, but also the most beautiful, the height of bullfighting. Right-hand passes are important, too, of course; controlling the bull and sculpting and fighting are done with the right, but the sword is always in the *muleta* with such passes and can extend it, a safer lure. The left hand is often called the "hand of gold," for artistic work can be done with the *muleta* at its smallest size. It is also said that it is the *muleta* that kills, not the sword. But it can't really be broken down into parts.

Comes a good, one-in-a-hundred bull, which can take good passes, and you can be artistic. You can keep a figure and apply a formula, like choreography in dancing, create a good *faena*. But you have to create a good *faena* even with a *manso*, a tricky bull, not brave. This is what takes knowledge—to get artistry out of a bad bull.

118

That's a *lidiador*. In three or four years I will tell whether or not I can be a good *lidiador*.

My training in music and art was beneficial to me. Sculpture can be very symbolic, and when you get that in a ring with your own body and bull and cape, it's art. Patience is most necessary, the realization that you have to work at something to make it evolve. It's intangible, but if you work at it hard enough and have genuine desire you'll develop it. It's more spiritual than physical; and, as El Gallo once said, you don't compete muscularly with a bull! Bullfighters have more in common with fine arts than athletes. A good one creates a beautiful *faena* by arranging a series of passes that are aesthetically and emotionally sound. That takes more knowledge and skill than muscular effort—and it must be created as the fight progresses.

I was back in Villa Acuña the fourth of July, after successive Sundays fighting in Reynosa, Piedra Negra and Juárez. I wanted to redeem myself after my first performance there, and besides that my mother had consented to come and see me again. Father found reasons for staying away. I cut two ears and felt somewhat better. Mother had a rough time though. The first bull was a *manso* and raised Holy Ned. He was a brindle, and Mother says she knew the moment she saw him come out I would have trouble. I went in over the horns for the kill and never got out, but it was a good thrust and he died without getting me. Mother said that it got her; she felt as if everything had gone out of her.

I waited for her in my hotel room after the fight. I finally finished my tea and hers and got bathed and dressed. She didn't show up until a couple of hours after the fight, and I was a little anxious and, perhaps, put out. She finally came with friends who had taken her to a bar to recuperate. The friends said she had actually shown pride in the things she had heard about me. One man had asked her if she knew me.

"She's my daughter!" was her answer.

I have never fought to my complete satisfaction in Villa Acuña, though it is one of the Border places which I like best. Mrs. Crosby always saves a big room, with a Spanish-type balcony, and there and in her restaurant I am made to feel like a queen. I love to go to the Macarena Cabaret in the open court before the bull ring for supper after the fight. Everybody is always so kind in Villa Acuña, including those friends from Del Rio across the border. I fought three times that first year in this atmosphere, some of the fights for the benefit of an international highway leading into Mexico, in which the chambers of commerce of both towns, the Mexican and the North American, cooperated. Only the river seems to divide those people, and that but little. I was glad to go back to Villa Acuña to fight in October.

We left for Mexico City right after the fight of the fourth of July to see about passport renewal and to be fitted for more clothes. It had been difficult to keep clothes in shape with all the travel and successive Sunday fights. Cleaning bills are one of the headaches of a matador, and often repair bills are added. Even when he is not hurt, he is usually bloodied if he passes the bull closely enough, and horns rip and tear even when they do not wound.

We were in Mexico City for two weeks. I think I went to two matinees; otherwise I only left the room to eat and for fittings. Alejandro was busy and I had to keep out of sight. I'd been besieged to fight in Mexico City, and Alejandro didn't want me to. The first offer had come in June, but the maestro didn't think I was ready, and he didn't want me to perform there as a novelty or a curiosity, but as a serious *torera*. He thought too many *novilleros* fought in the big plaza too soon and were too soon forgotten. He didn't want newsmen to interview me about this or any other phase of my career, though just before we left he allowed a couple of reporters to talk with me in the offices of the union.

That summer was one of trying to put together what had been learned through practice and what had been gained in actual fighting, learning to coordinate every movement until even my wrists functioned independently of thought. It was like studying scripts for a play, memorizing and practicing everything until it was right and natural. This matter of practice goes on all through the life of a matador. The great matadors, Ortega and Cagancho, who never have formally retired, still practice whether or not they are to fight. It is exciting just to think of it: *traje de luces* and white hair!

For a beginner everything can be a lesson. I could remember the fights in which I'd felt things right, and they were those in which I'd instinctively done the right thing. There isn't much time to think out procedures once the bull is being fought. If he is good he won't give you the time, in any case; each part of the body must instinctively cooperate to produce the right maneuver. In my third fight in Juárez, where I was practicing every day, I had tried to modify a pass after the bull had charged and he literally embraced and fell on top of me. I looked up and there he was staring at me, my head out behind his foreleg. His tongue was out, and I felt his hot breath panting in my face. He couldn't reach me, so we just looked at each other until the *banderilleros* got excited and tried to get him up. We'd have been better off if they'd left us alone, I thought. We'd have got up in time, but he knew where he had me.

In that same fight I caught the flow of the fight with the first pass. Things went so well and I was so sure of things that I knelt in front of the bull and handled his horns. When I reached for his ear he jumped at me, but he didn't hurt me. In other fights one sometimes has to offer himself more than the *muleta* as a target to get the animal to charge. No two are alike, though there seem to be similar habits in bulls of the same breed. There are certain traits one can expect from bulls of this or that ranch, and we always look for them in the first minutes of the fight, which is the only chance the matador has to study the bull from the sidelines. After a fight in Piedra Negra I once was presumptuous enough to think I knew bulls, but the next fight I learned that I didn't. And I remember a fight in Reynosa, because I discovered that some bulls can't be fought with low passes.

Alejandro was busy part of the summer arranging to get bulls from Don Tomás of El Valle in Chihuahua across the frontier for an exhibition in San Francisco. I knew about this, but I didn't know that it concerned me in any way until almost the middle of September, when we were over a hundred miles on our way to a fight in Nogales, when he announced that we wouldn't be back for about three weeks. He had told me to pack my bull-fighting clothes as we were going to Nogales to fight the following Sunday. I had included only enough clothes for a long week end.

I exclaimed about the "three weeks," and he said, "Certainly. We're going to California."

I thought he was joking, and he supposed that I knew all about it—how, I don't know, since I was not supposed to ask questions about business and he hadn't mentioned it. He became angry that I didn't have more clothes, adding insult to injury by asking me what I expected to wear for the television and radio shows in Tucson before the fight. Well, that was the first I had heard about that, too. So there was a big argument about my stupidity, and about his expecting me to be a mind reader. After the television show we practiced for a couple of days in the Nogales ring before the fight, and he was angry at everything I did. He wouldn't tell me what was wrong, so I felt pretty frustrated when the time for the fight arrived. It was then we started calling him *El Oso* (the bear).

He felt better about things after Don Pedro Gonzales, called Zángano (drone) by his friends, suggested the possibility of a mixed *corrida* for me. That would mean fighting with matadors *de toros*, and the idea was flattering coming from Zángano, who is an ex-bullfighter himself. He has seen the best, and to win his approval would mean something to me. He has always been friend and helper to me; he arranged for my inclusion in some of the *tientas* to which I had been invited. Zángano is one of whom they say, "He would still laugh with a knife stuck in his belly."

It was a good fight. I got the feeling of the bulls and finally could stretch out, chin tucked in, legs and feet planted, and lean forward and guide the bull. It really is like stretching, reaching for freedom, like opening the doors of freedom, knowing you have control and can make the fight artistic and emotional. Before that it is think, think, think.

I gave the bulls a few right-hand passes, ending in *pasos de pecho,* opening the door for them and wrapping them around me. It is a great spiritual satisfaction. It meant more to me than the time I got four ears and two tails. And these were bulls which the matador Hector Saucedo had seen while on his way to fight somewhere with Carlos Arruza. He had thought them too big for me, and he told me that no woman should be in a ring with *novillos* of that size.

"Well, they're dead now," I told him.

Because bullfighting is an art and a science, there's no reason for distinction between sexes. Bulls charge man or woman alike. The same skill is necessary in either case, and the public pays for a good performance regardless. There is no law in Mexico (contrary to a recent statement by Sidney Franklin) about the size of bulls for women. I have equal chances with the men in the *sorteo* where representatives of the matadors draw lots for their enemies of the afternoon. Great fighters, like Arruza, can demand good bulls. Size is not the most important element. Small bulls charge faster and turn more quickly, and they can give as severe a goring. A good *torero* can fight any size.

Zángano and his partner were so pleased with my fight that, though it was Sunday night, they had a jewelry store opened and told me to select anything I wished to have. I chose a dainty little medal, but Alejandro wouldn't let me accept it; he insisted that I choose a watch.

We drove from Nogales to Hollister, California, where there is a large Spanish colony. The bulls from El Valle were already there, eleven of them in charge of a caretaker. Fighting bulls are always under the care of a man from their ranch until they actually fight. There were two other *novilleros* and another *banderillero* waiting for us. A wooden corral had been built to take the place of a bull ring. Of course there could be no real *corrida* in California. Instead, the simulated fight or *capea* would follow the outlines of a bullfight, except that no *pics* would be used, *banderillas* would be pointless and barbless, and at the "kill" the hand was placed on the unwounded spot as though following a sword in to the hilt. The people were all excited, in spite of the fact that it couldn't be a real *corrida*. They wanted to see some of the art of the festival, even if it must be deprived of much of the drama and emotion. Of course it would be more dangerous for the matadors, for we had to use the cape and *muleta* and try to get over the horns as though to kill, without the preparation that makes these acts possible and good to watch.

When I took the aluminum practice sword to use in the folds of the *muleta* for *ayudados* (passes in which the sword extends and stiffens the *muleta*), a distinguished-looking gentleman detained me. "I thought you weren't going to use swords," he said.

I had to explain that it was a practice sword, one with which you could hardly hurt a bull if you tried. This was my first contact with a member of the Humane Society. They were breathing down our necks all the time we were in California, as they had indirectly when I had made the TV appearance the previous January. At that time I had been charged with trying to introduce bull-fighting into the United States.

When we moved on to San Francisco, they had someone watching us all the time, I think. I remember a woman who tried to pet one of the bulls in the corral, promising that she wouldn't let us hurt one hair of his cute little head—all in baby talk—until he tried to hook her right through the corral.

After they saw how ornery the bulls were, some of the Humane Society people started worrying about us. They wanted to know what made us want to get into the ring with such ill-tempered beasts.

The *capea* in Hollister went off all right, even with all the simulation. We were then taken to a feast, all the *toreros* at one table. I ate so much they asked me where I kept it all. There was folk dancing and regular dancing and a continuous barbecue all afternoon and night. I had to go on a diet after I got home or I might have justified the remark someone made while I was eating —that I'd look like a lady wrestler if I didn't watch out.

Since there had been only eleven bulls, we had to use one over again at the Cow Palace the next week in San Francisco. No bull is ever supposed to be fought a second time; he learns so much in his first that he is almost impossible to fight in a second appearance. He is quite apt to kill the matador. This second fight for one bull almost broke up the show, and is what chiefly got the Humane Society people worrying about humans for a change. Alejandro and the other *banderillero* almost lost their pants.

Alejandro had been showing some really beautiful passes with the cape when the bull turned suddenly and hoisted him from behind, so that Alejandro's seat and back were on the horns. I was the first to reach them, and when Alejandro got off, I took the bull away with my cape. The crowd was so pleased to see the disciple rescue the master that there was an instant of silence before the roar of yelling and clapping. There could have been a ridiculous moment if I had not refused to do fancy passes; I simply held the bull at bay until Alejandro recovered and could finish his own *quites*.

Alejandro likes to tell this on me. I had already known that *quites* to rescue another *torero* are not always in the good faith they may appear to be; they are sometimes used to outdisplay the unfortunate one being rescued. I had no thought of doing anything fancy; this was my childish way of showing understanding and respect, with honor, to my maestro.

The people of the Humane Society ended by asking for autographed pictures of all of us.

There were amusing incidents during our stay in San Francisco. Of course we all wanted to see the sights. The first time out I had insisted on getting the tickets for the excursion, since I supposedly spoke the best English. We wound up going toward the outskirts of Oakland. So we saw Chinatown, Golden Gate, the bridges, and Fisherman's Wharf by taxi. When we were about to get tickets for the boat tour of the Bay, Alejandro insisted on getting them "so we won't wind up in Korea." But he got tickets, not for the large ship we wanted to board, but for a little tugboat.

We had to hurry a little to get back for the Villa Acuña fight, the fifth of October. From there I went home to Big Spring for a week to plan my wardrobe for the *tientas*. It was a good week. I went to shows with my folks; I played records to my heart's content. I listened to the Metropolitan Opera over the air and generally did just as I pleased. But toward the end of the week I got restless for the bulls.

Back in Juárez it was practice and practice as we waited for the *tientas*. It seemed to me they were eternally being postponed. There was a pleasant interlude in the visit of Anna Beatrice Cuchette, the *rejoneadora* from Columbia, and her father. He was busy training horses for her to use in the ring, since they had been unable to bring theirs from South America. I spent a lot of time with her. Señor Cuchette wanted to show me points about riding, but Alejandro wouldn't let me even mount. He said my business was on foot. (Only recently has he let me drive a car.) I enjoyed Anna's company very much; though she fought from horseback, we had much in common.

The day before my birthday, November 18, Alejandro bought a new Lincoln. We spent my birthday breaking it in, driving as far as Arizona. We had the new car for driving to the *tientas* and felt quite smart with it. A few days later we left for Aguascalientes, and stayed at the Francia. I was as excited as the first time. The town was full of matadors, *novilleros*, and aspirants. My first visit was to my old friends the Duques.

Seven

Las Tientas

Tienta is translated in one dictionary as "sagacity in finding something out." What are called *tientas* in the world of bullfighting are tests where all the sagacity and acumen of the *ganaderos,* as the breeders of fighting bulls are called, are brought to bear on determining as far as possible how brave the bulls of the *ganadería* (ranch) will be two years later and in the generations to come. That they also provide experience for *toreros,* sport for *aficionados,* and occasions for social festivity is really incidental.

Ganaderos are extremely anxious to have the bulls which wear the ranch colors into the plazas give good accounts of themselves. Famous bulls are discussed, their mounted heads displayed prominently, and their names mentioned almost reverently. The reputation of a ranch is based on the proportion of its noble bulls who have thus distinguished themselves. If *pundonor* in a matador is the sense of obligation to do his best with the integrity expected of him, in the *ganadero* it is sending brave, well-built, properly bred and developed bulls to the ring. The testing of his animals and the recording of each detail in the book in which the ancestry of each animal is kept are of prime importance to the *ganadero*. He will direct the tests himself, determining which two-year-old bulls will be "*toro*" and which will be "oxen" or meat and which heifers will mother fighting bulls and which will go the way to the slaughterhouse.

Matadors, invited by the *ganadero* to take part in his *tienta*, attend out of friendship, for the practice provided, and the pleasure involved. One might almost say that a good *tienta*, with top matadors testing, is similar to a jam session among topflight musicians; they are performing with those who know, indulging the pleasures of skill and craftsmanship.

Other invited guests usually include amateur *toreros* from business and the professions, those who are not professional bullfighters, but who enjoy the art and like to try a hand with the cape. Some of these are very good and some provide great sport for the other guests. These also add to the social gaiety which prevails when the actual testings are not being conducted.

Then there are always hopeful apprentices, *novilleros*, and others seeking recognition as well as practice with live animals.

In addition to those participating in the tests, there are usually a number of other guests and relatives on hand for the occasion. Distinguished journalists, perhaps artists, people of the theater, and a priest or two may be among the audience which silently (noise at testings is taboo) watch the art or the sport as animal after animal is let into the small ring to challenge the picador on horseback and, it is hoped, continue challenging time after time. If it is a cow, she will charge the capes and *muletas* also until the *ganadero* happily cries "*toro*," or disgustedly mutters "oxen," if she is laggard in the attack. There are always girls and women among the watchers and in the *salons* when the work is done, cousins and friends of the daughters and family. All these add to the social aspects of the *tientas*.

Besides the honor of being invited, I was grateful for the practice and what I learned watching those more expert than I and listening to their comments. Bulls are the basis of the art and the more one knows about them the better artist he is apt to be in the *corrida*, and the place to learn is certainly on the *ganaderías*, whose reason for existence is the breeding of fighting bulls and without which the strains cared for and developed over the centuries would weaken and die out. More care has gone into the breeding of fighting bulls than into beef or dairy cattle and for a much longer time, for conformation, horn, and bravery, as well as style of charge, are necessary factors in the fighting bull.

Tientas for young bullfighters might be likened to examinations before a board of experts. Those watching notice and discuss and judge the newcomers and *novilleros* and may talk about them later. They may be offered valuable advice, and they may learn qualities that go to make the matadors skillful or artistic. Performing in *tientas* combines, for me, the results of the past year's fighting with the promise of the year to come, and the chance to study others and absorb the knowledge that is available.

To a North American, going to many of the *tientas* may also be like dropping back into the historic past. Certainly the first two *tientas* in which I was fortunate to participate that season of 1952-1953 were in settings that might have been lifted from the pages of Cervantes. To a person like me, who has always been somewhat romantic, these "castles" and the history behind them recalled all the ideas of knightly adventure that had so occupied my childhood dreams, and they were tied in intimately with bullfighting.

To make the contrast keener, part of our journey to this past (that has all the conveniences for modern, gracious living) was made by plane from Mexico City to San Luis Potosí. Zángano was with us, and the famous matador, Manuel Capetillo, who was also going to the *tienta* at Las Garfias. He and I were to alternate in testing the cows, which added to the romance—sharing cows with a full matador instead of taking them later.

Capetillo arrived at the Mexico City airport early. I was reading a magazine when he came up. The old shyness came over me. I self-consciously tried to act poised, not hold my hands clumsily, and all that, so I pretended to be interested in the magazine. When we were on the plane I got up courage enough to offer to share my chocolate bars. He put one in his pocket, and then I was afraid he would let it melt.

It was a night flight of perhaps an hour or two. Javier, the eldest Garfias son, who was in charge of the hacienda, met us at the plane in San Luis and drove us to the beautiful town home of the Garfias family for a brief rest and then on to the hacienda. The road wound through mountains and across dams and through valleys until a sudden turn brought us to the gates of a walled village. In the center of the village another wall surrounded the hacienda proper, Las Garfias. I was taken to a large bedroom where the moon shone in the window. I could hear the lowing of cattle outside. I could hardly sleep in the rich atmosphere.

About five o'clock in the morning I heard *vaqueros* bringing in herds. I sat up in bed, though it was chilly, and a creepy feeling came over me, thinking of the cows I would fight before a critical audience. I suppose it was a little anxiety about how I would perform, and probably a little fear, a little self-distrust. I remembered a long time ago, when I was a kid in Kansas, when cowboys riding ahead of a herd approached and we could see the clouds of dust; the feeling of excitement as we'd run for a closer look and then try to hide; how I'd finally wish I were one of the men on horseback, helping, or a matador saving someone by caping a mad bull that had strayed; the screams of the kids, "Here they come!"; and all the imaginings before the herd passed, bawling and mooing, and finally the strays.

But I didn't fight that first day. It was too windy to use the capes. We drove out to see the bulls in the pastures, in their separate herds. I was interested in two that locked horns and sort of wrestled Indian fashion. All in that herd were restless, though they seemed to recognize the *ganadero*. We had to approach them very quietly and speak very low, climbing up over a hump of wooded ground. These were *novillos*, three to four years old, around a water trough. We walked back as quietly —not from fear, but to refrain from disturbing the bulls, who should finally arrive at a ring with as little experience as possible with men on foot. I thought they seemed to be doing very well for bachelors, for the only cows that fighting bulls remember are their mothers. Imagine, and then perhaps to be killed by a woman!

At this first *tienta* the men tested some of the two-year-old bulls, though not with capes. Each was let into the miniature ring where a mounted picador waited with his testing *pic*. The good bulls immediately charged the padded horse and continued the attack until distracted by a man behind the barrier showing himself and calling "ha! ha!" to induce the bull to leave the horse. When the man disappeared, most of the brave, stubborn creatures renewed the attack on the horse in spite of the punishment of the *pic*, which is painful, though not as damaging as the *pics* used in a *corrida*. I watched all of this with the women of the hacienda and their guests. We had to be very quiet, and I was restless waiting for the cows.

The ladies of the family and their friends were very kind to the North American girl. They enjoyed discussing the things all women like; they are always interested in American clothes, since theirs follow European patterns more than ours do. They judge by quality more than by fads. I dressed simply; I always wear skirts long (because of my long legs) regardless of Paris, and I travel in a suit. Sweaters intrigue them, and I generally take a few to *tientas,* as many of the haciendas are high in altitude and can be cold.

"In your country women command the men," they'd often say, and I'd find myself defending North American men, though I'm certainly not an expert on the subject.

I was shy at first and didn't want to intrude on the men and their talk about bulls, though my chief interests lay there. I'd play dominoes or canasta with the women in the afternoons. In the evening everyone gathered in the *salon.* There were huge fireplaces at each end, and portraits of bullfighters, brands of different ranches, and the heads of famous bulls on the walls. Sometimes guitars were strummed, or groups of people sat around and talked. One afternoon I missed a serenade by Capetillo, who has a beautiful voice, because I was having so much fun in the shower. It was natural hot water and I'd had trouble getting it running correctly until several people in turn showed me how. It was so wonderful that I stayed in, once it got going, and serenaded myself with Puccini arias until I was as wrinkled as a prune.

One of the portraits in the salon was of Conchita Cintron by Llopes. It was a beautiful picture. I liked to hear them speak of her; she had been at the hacienda and was liked and admired by one and all. The next morning her name came up again at breakfast. Her fighting was discussed and her good work commended to such an extent that I felt like finishing my coffee under the table. I felt that I was to be compared with her, a polished artist, while I was a mere beginner. That was like comparing a green *novillero* to a *gran* matador *de toros.* I had so enjoyed hearing about her the night before, but in the morning it brought the butterflies to my interior. (However, I later felt that I had passed my grades.)

I alternated with Capetillo. I was very happy that what I had learned with Alejandro worked out well with the cows. With one cow I fought particularly well, even doing a *molinete* and other involved passes. But most pleasure came from being able to use the form I'd been taught.

Everyone rushed over to congratulate Alejandro, though some shook my hand as they passed me. I was left with the cow, which was just as well since I was shy with praise and thus had a chance to make an exit. When I was behind the barrier Capetillo congratulated me and asked, incredulously, if I were positive that no Spanish blood flowed in my veins. He was most generous. Of course the main thrill was to have pleased the *ganadero*, Don Javier, with the way I handled his cows. Again the feeling of breaking out of walls, that stretching to freedom, that spiritual satisfaction. Confidence. A foothold in the struggle, that is most of living, to find meaning and power within myself.

There were games with cocktails and at dinner. In one game everyone was supposed to write down the first thought which came to his mind. I was so elated that I wrote, "You are the way you spend your time."

I fought again the next day, another good one for me. Zángano kept shouting, "Give her a big cow!"

More guests came for dinner that night, among whom were Señor and Señora Meade Diez Guiterrez, owners of La Ventilla. They invited me to a *tienta* at their *ganadería,* to be held in the near future. We had to leave for Mexico City the next morning, but I promised to be at the La Ventilla *tienta!*

In Mexico City, as usual, I had a small dark room. But we dressed well and drove a Lincoln! I spent most of my time in the room, hoping for definite *tienta* dates. I never knew until Alejandro would come and say, "Get packed. Today we leave for a *tienta.*"

We were back in San Luis Potosí within a week, but we had to wait a day before flying to La Ventilla. I had a spacious room in the beautiful hotel, with a huge window overlooking the picturesque old town; but I got restless as I always do when waiting, so I practiced with the *muleta* in the room. (Often in smaller hotels I've practiced fighting the bull standing on the bed.) After dinner that night I was allowed to go to a show, but it was a depressing drama. I was still depressed the next morning.

I dressed for fighting, as I thought we were coming back to the hotel that night, and Alejandro was furious. I had to change and pack all my things. This didn't help my low mood. I felt that the *tienta* was ruined before it had started. He nagged me so often that I told him it was a good thing he wasn't a woman; any man would have divorced him. It was all very exhausting.

We took a small private plane to La Ventilla. We had to wait at the airport a little while, and I noticed Carlos Arruza, the great Mexican matador, and his beautiful young Spanish wife with a group of people. Alejandro brought one of the men over and introduced him as the Peruvian matador, Alejandro Montani. I had a piece of a chocolate bar in my mouth, my hair was down, and I was almost on the point of tears because of my maestro's constant scolding.

"*Mucho gusto,* matadora," Montani said, politely enough. "With much pleasure, matadora."

I don't remember what I said, but I was overly sensitive, I guess, because I thought I detected sarcasm in the "matadora." I thought, I'll show him, sometime, that I deserve the title in terms of what it literally means. I didn't know then that he had a reputation as a good killer. He had been fighting in Spain, and I hadn't heard of him before this meeting. He was most distinguished looking and stockier than many of the matadors I'd met. I was curious about him and asked Alejandro. Alejandro told me to tend to business, that if I didn't straighten out he wouldn't take me to any more *tientas.* I replied that there'd be some pleasure in that, since in that case it would be the last *tienta* with him. (He told me about Montani later.)

The plane circled the ranch and I looked down on what really appeared to be a castle, complete with towered church at one corner, great central patio, and courts and wings, all of stone. It was most intriguing. We circled the small *tienta* ring and saw a truck leave it for the airstrip. The truck arrived just as we landed and we were met by the *dueño,* called *El Gordo,* who took us to the great house for breakfast and introductions to the family and friends. I remember a bride who stuck close to her husband. I particularly liked the vivacious daughter, Emma, and her friend, Pita Ponte de Santos, who later gave me a medal of the Virgin of Carmen, which I always wear in the ring. I spent most of my time with Emma and Pita when not fighting. Emma had been to school in St. Louis, where I was born. The gracious way these people put us at our ease, as though they had known us for years, made a deep impression. I had a corner room on the second floor, reached by a ramp, in lieu of stairs, from the great central patio.

We were shown the stables and drove out a little way from the buildings, where I watched a fighting heifer playing with an ordinary bull calf of the same age. She was much too rough for him, had more horn and spunk. He'd run off to his mother, come back to stare at her a moment before trying to play again, and soon run back to his mother again. The heifer was like an experienced boxer and pushed him around. Every time he lost ground she'd take advantage of it to give him a good butt or hook. "The difference in blood," someone said.

The old father teased me at the dinner table. He said it was interesting to meet a lady who fought bulls, and a North American at that.

"I have always wanted a matador in my family," he said. "And with twelve children I have none, while your parents hit the jackpot with one!"

Choir boys sang the service in the church which projected from a corner of the patio. I say church; actually it reminded me of a small cathedral. A good life, that on an old hacienda; fine people, good friends; enough of the serious things of life and pleasure and sport too, all seemingly in perfect proportions. No wonder I want to be a *ganadero* when I retire from the ring.

When we were back at the airport in San Luis, waiting for the Mexico City plane, newsmen caught me before I could get inside the station out of the cold. They asked all sorts of questions, including when I would fight in

San Luis. I didn't know what to answer about anything, since Alejandro is touchy about interviews. I begged to go inside. There I immediately saw Carlos Arruza and his wife again. If I'd had any feelings of pride about being waited on by the press, they were dissipated. It was Arruza who'd brought them out; I was only the second run.

From Mexico City I went home for Christmas with gifts which had been bought from my own earnings for the first time. It was a great pleasure to be able to do just that little thing. It's still fun to look back at the things the bulls got for me and to be financially independent—in a way.

As usual I got in a little partying at home, including a New Year's Eve date at the country club. I went with a nice, young jet pilot, Bill Rice, who was a friend of the family. I enjoyed the change for a while—before becoming restless again for the bulls.

One thing one can be certain of with any given *tienta* is the uncertainty as to just when it is to be held. Invitations may be given a year in advance for the hacienda's *tienta*, but no date will be set exactly. Weather is one factor, and another may be the availability of the principal matadors invited; but another is to keep the knowledge of the time from the hordes of young aspirants, each hoping for a chance to practice and, if lucky, draw attention to himself by crashing a *tienta*. Even if he does have a chance in a *tienta* ring, his cow will be *toreada* (previously fought) and consequently smart and very dangerous. Often, if they are permitted in the ring with such a cow, it is to provide sport for the onlookers, who have perhaps just seen a great matador perform artistically and well with a fresh cow.

I went to the *tienta* of Santo Domingo in San Luis Potosí in December, 1953, just about a year after the La Ventilla *tienta*. I think I have never seen so many aspirants in one place before. Even the invited guests amounted to such a crowd that finally they put the women on one side of the huge house and the men on the other. I don't know where all the young aspirants slept—I suppose in the stables or other out buildings, and I suppose they were able to eat in the kitchens. I did not feel very well all during that *tienta* (which was prolonged from day to day by weather), and I had great sympathy for the hardships these boys endure and their aspirations.

How they learn about *tienta* dates is a mystery, but boys from various parts of the country arrive at most of them, tired and hungry from walking or hitchhiking long distances. You'll see them in twos and threes along the highways of Mexico, usually dressed in blue jeans or khaki pants tied high at the waist with the unmistakable sign of the profession, the narrow, woven *charro* tie used as a belt. They will have a cap pulled over one eye and a dirty bundle containing capes and *palillos* (notched sticks which hold the *muletas*) swung over their shoulders on another stick, which may be a wooden practice sword. They tramp cross-country on dusty roads during the heat of the day, and at night they try to keep warm by rolling up in their fighting capes wherever they have found a grove of trees or other likely place to sleep. Often they reach a *tienta* and never have a chance to test their skill and prowess at all. Perhaps they can hear talk that is informative from a *gana-dero* or a matador and see the experts in action; perhaps they can learn somehow of the time and place of another *tienta* and set out once more with hope and ambition for fuel to keep them going. Of course not all serious aspirants are poor boys trying to emulate the lives of matadors like Manolete and Belmonte who rose from abject poverty to fame and fortune. (There is a saying in Spain that the only way to be rich is to be born a nobleman or to become a successful matador.) There are matadors and young aspirants from all classes in Mexico.

There was a fine-looking young man at Santo Domingo *tienta* who came with the uninvited but who wore *campero* (the Andalusian pants that fall to a few inches above the ankle, and which are split at the cuff to allow silver ornaments to be inserted in their buttonholes), the costume of the well-dressed gentleman at *tientas*. He was no ordinary boy in his teens, as were his companions with whom he seemed to be popular. He was also unusual in that he was a tease and not quiet, almost timid, in the presence of the *ganadero* as most of the *novilleros* seem to be.

The *ganadero* and some of his *aficionado* friends got to wondering about this boy and asked him about his background and whether or not he was serious about becoming a bullfighter. The young man said that he had left his studies as a medical student in order to try to fulfill his consuming desire to fight the bulls as a professional. He wanted to pursue his ambition as the other aspirants do, going without food and water on long trips to *tientas* to which he had not been invited.

The *ganadero*, Don Manuel Labastida, uttered a long despairing groan.

"Go back to school," he said. "Go back to school."

It was the first time I had seen the *ganadero* express any emotion. He meant what he said; that was evident. And the fine lady, the Señora de Labastida, sighed and shook her head.

The boy had a proud face, if not too confident a manner. He could not conceal his disappointment at hearing these words from the respected *ganadero*. I was for him, myself, but I knew what was in the mind of Don Manuel and his friends. For every one that makes it, there are countless boys who never get a chance, and numbers of others who are crippled in limb or in courage before they approach the top. And to be a doctor in Mexico is very good. It is a highly respected profession. I could feel the loneliness of the young ex-student as he walked away, and I remembered my own luck and was grateful for it.

Perhaps the boy had read of de la Serna who left the medical profession to become one of Spain's outstanding matadors. I understand that de la Serna still practices medicine in Spain, since his retirement from the ring. He also had followed the bulls on his own initiative and against his family's wishes. There is a *muleta* pass named after him, the *la sernista*.

It may have been the weather which aided the aspirants in reaching this Santo Domingo *tienta* before it was concluded. Certainly rain caused the actual testing to be postponed from day to day, even after most of the participants had arrived. When there was a dry day, the ground in the ring was so wet that fires of straw were burned over it to try to dry it out enough for good footing—mostly in vain. I would have enjoyed the festivities that filled in the interludes had I not felt ill most of the time. As it was, I did poorly with the cows I fought. My head was pounding and I couldn't seem to do the right thing. I was particularly sorry since I followed the great maestro Fermin Espinosa Armillita, who had retired but has reappeared this last year again as a matador. He knew how to handle even the most difficult little cow.

There was no lack of action between testings. We organized ball teams and played in the great first patio between the arched veranda of the house and the church; we set up a pistol range in another patio. (I aimed at one of three cans on a wall and hit the one on the opposite end from that at which I had aimed.) We went rabbit shooting by truck. (I had better luck there when my turn came to stand in front of the others and shoot at rabbits scared up as the truck zigzagged over the terrain.) The young girls serenaded at all hours or followed the popular Jesús Córdoba, who had just returned from a successful season in Spain. Finally all the girls (I was included with the teen-agers since I was unmarried) had to sleep in beds made up on the floor of the study. It was really crowded. I got little sleep, since this was a gala event for the girls, and each night was a slumber party.

At dinner I sat next to Armillita, whom I had met earlier in the year. Before the maestro I was as shy as a girl on her first date. (I recently saw him fight in Mexico City, and he is more of an idol to me than ever.) After dinner there were more songs, more games, and more stories.

I felt so miserable one night that I thought I'd sneak off and try to get some sleep before the teen-agers went to bed. So I went tearing into the study without knocking, thinking the beds would be made up on the floor and that everyone else was in the *salon*. The beds were ready, but the timing was a little off, and I stumbled into a discussion among Don Manuel, Armillita, and some of their friends. There was a fire in the hearth at the end of the room, but each of the men had on a heavy, colorful poncho, his head stuck up through the slit in the middle. I was as surprised as I was embarrassed. After I'd apologized, they asked me to stay, and when the maestro himself urged me to sit down and talk, I did stay. That was the highlight of the whole *tienta* for me. Listening to their talk and the serious undertones when they spoke of certain bulls and fighters and methods, I soon felt at ease with them. I imagined to myself that someday I would know enough to enter into such conversations; that someday I might be a *ganadero*, with my own bulls and knowledge of them and concerns about their breeding. The mystery of the *Fiesta Brava* was present even here, away from the triumphs and failures of the ring. Before the high priests, I felt like a devotee, learning of the mysteries and rites of a great ceremony. The only light in the room came from the great fire casting light and shadow on the walls and on the faces of the talkers, huddled in their *ponchos*. I was proud just to be with them, a member of the fraternity to which they and the famous men pictured on the walls belonged.

147

The kind Señora de Labastida asked me to share a room with two young señoras so that I could rest better and perhaps feel more up to par in the morning. To my surprise, I awakened when it was light to find I'd been alone in the room all night. I got up early and grabbed a bathroom to myself. It was raining again. We were to leave that day since Alejandro and Jesús Córdoba were to fight the next Sunday in Irapuato. Armillita suggested to my teacher that I stay at the hacienda in case of further testing, since I didn't feel too well, instead of making the trip with them. I was pleased, certainly, but hardly hopeful. Alejandro agreed. It's wonderful what a great man can do! What I liked best from then on was looking up the ancestry and records of the little cows we were to fight, in the books of the *ganaderías*. The history of the hacienda itself is to be found in these records that go back to the first introduction of fighting-bull blood. I was told that every young bullfighter who aspires to the top of his profession should study the bulls as though he intended to raise them. To learn something about fighting bulls from his own experience is one of the intense satisfactions a bullfighter can have; but there is much to be gained that can be learned only in the history of the breeding. This discovery leads to skill as well as art and knowledge and has always meant much to me. I've said this before but I repeat it because it is so important to me.

As the bull ring is the ultimate reason for the *ganaderías*, as it is where the matador displays the best that is in him, so the *tientas* are for a period of both development and trial. Probably most of the people, at least along the Border, who attend the *corridas*, don't

Above: Bowing before the authorities at the conclusion of the parade.

At left: Sculpting, out of the ring.

Above: Orticina, a pass named after Pepe Ortiz, at the *corrida* of Easter, 1953. *Below:* Triumphal tour of the ring, with awards for a good fight.

Pase de pecho (chest pass):

First step

Second step

Third step

At left: "The La Punta bull that got me," a *novillo o* 340 kilos.

Below: Patricia lets the bull pass so close that he almost stumbles over her foot. *(United Press Photo)*

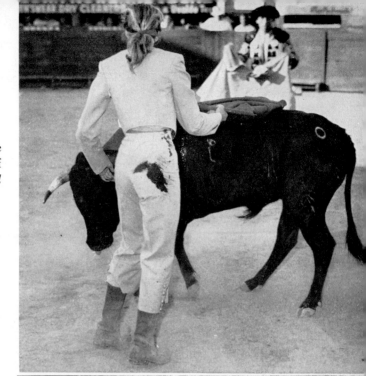

blood of the
is a badge of
age. *(United
s Photo)*

icia McCormick
y evades the
s horns as she
for a fatal stab
the sharp *es-
. (United Press
o)*

Above: She almost falls as the bull lunges at her. *(United Press Photo)*

Below: This time Patricia is really down! She got up quickly and successfully fought the bull to the finish. *(United Press Photo)*

to Domingo bull:

Gaonera

Veronica

Pase por alto

Patricia McCormick gets the bull's ear after her first kill.

Patricia McCormick.

realize how much thought and effort go into the breeding and selection of fighting-bull stock, any more than such people understand what has brought a matador to his moment of glory or the path he has traveled to defeat and possible destruction in the ring. *Tientas* make one realize that bulls don't naturally grow that way and, I might add, allow *toreros* to develop skills and gain knowledge under more auspicious conditions than they can always find under the regulations of a *corrida*.

And I would say to any North American—or Mexican, for that matter—that if you are ever fortunate enough to be invited to a *tienta* at one of the great haciendas, by all means, go. You will discover much about the art of the brave festival that prejudices may have prevented your understanding before. And you will meet wonderful people! It's your own fault if you don't have one of the best times of your life.

Eight

Baptism of Blood

I have skipped almost a year's time jumping from the *tienta* of La Ventilla to that of Santo Domingo. Perhaps it was because that year, my second as a professional, was less of triumphs than of pain and doubt. Not that I had less determination in my desires, but I did have the pain; the doubts were natural in any case, and in a sense I triumphed, for I am still fighting.

I went home for Christmas, and I had been hoping for a date to a *tienta* at the *ganadería* of Pepe Ortiz, the great retired matador who has always been the chief idol in my pantheon of Mexican matadors. My friend Zángano had promised that I would be invited, and I was on tenterhooks for days, waiting for the confirmation of the date. Alejandro called the day before New Year's Day, 1953, to tell me to leave on that day, and then he called again to postpone it. Since I was as eager to meet the great Ortiz as to fight his cows and the delays made me irritable, the New Year got off to a bad start. I learned on the first that I would not fight in Juárez on the eighteenth of January. There had been talk of a *corrida* there at that time to celebrate my anniversary as a *novillero*. There were other dates set for me to fight, but I had wanted this anniversary fight, perhaps only for romantic reasons, and when it was not to be mine I could think only of the Pepe Ortiz *tienta*.

When we did get started for that *tienta* and got as far as Aguascalientes, we discovered that it had been held. There had been some mix-up in the telegrams, and they had waited for us for two days before going ahead with the testing. So we were in no hurry to leave Aguascalientes and called on Dr. and Señora Duque, intending to leave the next day for Mexico City. We then decided to stay at the hotel over the week end.

On Monday morning, Don Juan Bilbao, of the Juárez ring, arrived at the hotel with Alejandro Montani, who had called me matadora at the San Luis airport when we met, and who I now learned was one of the matadors who were to fight in Juárez on the eighteenth. I still hoped for a chance to make him use the term without the slightest trace of the sarcasm which I had at least imagined had been in his tone; and I was irked that he had a place I'd wanted in the Juárez *corrida*. Of course he was a full matador and I was silly, since it was not his fault that he had been billed where

I wanted to be. He probably didn't know that I had any-thing to do with it. Alejandro, my teacher, says that jealousy is necessary in the ring, and I guess I felt it then, outside of the ring. At least I was envious. At the same time I was attracted to Montani. He looked like a strong character, had a nice, sensitive mouth, and was most courteous. I could see that he was trying to meas-ure me, too. (I often think, when I meet matadors, how like a zoo it is. The monkeys seem to size up the people as much as the people look at the monkeys.)

When Montani came in, I had been deviling Don Enrique Gonzales to take me to his brother Don Ra-miro's ranch to see a couple of baby bulls that had been taken into the hacienda to nurse since they had lost their mothers. A little later we were asked to test some cows of La Punta, one of the famous *ganaderías* of Mexico. There would be just Montani and me. I was pleased about this but still pensive over my bad luck with the Juárez *corrida*.

I was sitting in the hotel lobby, staring into space and thinking of the *tientas* I had missed, wondering how many cows poorer I was, when Montani, whom I hadn't noticed sitting across from me, spoke.

"*¿Preocupado* [preoccupied], *señorita?*"

"*Sí*," I answered abruptly.

A few minutes later Zángano, who had been confiden-tial *banderillero* to Ortiz, came over and said he had talked by telephone with Pepe Ortiz and that the latter had promised me a few cows to test. I was so happy then that I regretted my curt answer to the Peruvian matador.

Montani spent his time in the lobby while the other men kept coming and going. Later on I went upstairs and, as I looked back, caught his eye. I thought I'd better smile for a change, and I did. He smiled back. I turned away for a minute but when I looked back he was still smiling. I thought, all I have to do now is show him in the *tienta* that I'm a matadora and the thought of him won't bother me any more. Just before I went out of sight he was still looking up at me. I had gone up to change to a sweater, and when I came down again the girl at the desk complimented me on it so loudly that I became embarrassed and half ran to the street, where I was very angry with myself over my girlish shyness. Surely, I thought, I ought to be old enough to overcome that trait.

When we went to Fausto's, the restaurant attached to the hotel, Alejandro told me that since we might fight that afternoon I had better not eat the full-course dinner, which I easily could have enjoyed. I looked over and saw that Montani was enjoying "the works," but I didn't mention this to my maestro.

We still had to wait after dinner, so I went upstairs to rest, leaving the door of the room open so I wouldn't miss the first indication that we were ready to go. I dozed off in half-sleep, and as if in a dream I heard someone say, "Hello." After the second hello I thought it was some *aficionado*, and I was going to pretend sleep in earnest. But when there was a third hello I turned and shouted hello back.

It was Montani! I jumped up and fumbled around, looking for a hat, asking him if they were ready.

"No, no," he said. "Don't be alarmed. There is much time." Then he left with an apology for startling me.

I waited a few minutes before going downstairs. I

was still drugged from sleep when I got into one of the two vehicles which were to take us to La Punta. I was curious about the ranch from which such well-reputed bulls come. I was introduced to Don Pepe. Don Paco, his brother, was absent. I waited alone on the veranda until I almost fell asleep, so I went back to the car and tried to stay awake. Finally the others came and we drove along a lane, through groves of trees, to the ring where ten cows awaited the attentions of Montani and me.

For some reason I did not have the elation I had had at other *tientas* when about to meet the cows. It annoyed me. The cows had lots of temperament, too. For the first time I had to do the work of a peon and help run the cows, to see how they take the cape. Ordinarily I'd have enjoyed that experience. I blamed the holidays at home and the nearly ten pounds of extra weight they had put on me. (I'm at my best at 122 pounds.) I became exhausted quickly, and this gave me a little self-doubt.

When it came to the testing, Montani took the most difficult cows, politely letting me have the best, but even so I was sluggish and the cows were too smart. They kept me running in circles after them, calling out "ha! ha!" and slapping my hip smartly, trying to incite a charge.

"Why don't you make *veronicas* like Montani?" Alejandro kept yelling when I was trying to cape the animals.

When he called, "*¿Tiene miedo* [have you fear]?" it was the last straw.

"Yes, I'm afraid. So what?" I yelled back.

I looked up and Montani was smiling at Don Pepe and Don Ramiro. Again I remembered the "matadora" at the airport. I wasn't afraid; I was angry at myself and felt ridiculous and humiliated. I'd show them something—that I can fight well, and am serious. I gave Montani a determined glance as I exchanged my cape for the sword and *muleta*. I wasn't pretty—I was sweaty, disheveled, and dirty, but I was going to fight that cow properly, come hell or high water. She was the last of the day, a treacherous cow who learned very quickly.

I measured my steps toward her. I didn't care how temperamental or smart she was. I planted my feet uncompromisingly and offered fight.

She must have understood my determination, for she took the cape and did what I wanted her to do. I had to fight her very close to make her do it, even crossing her to make her think a charge worth her while. She took two high passes, and I went across her to make her charge on the right. She took two beautifully and by the third, she knew—but she didn't let me know she knew. She charged for the *muleta* and just as she reached it, turned and hooked me inside of the right thigh. It felt like a bee sting as I was lifted up and tossed to the ground. As she stomped on me, I put my arm over my head, waiting for her to quit or be taken off so I could get up and finish with her.

Montani caped her away from me. I got up and found my *muleta* and sword, feeling a little dizzy. Then I felt a draft and looked down to see if I was decent. My pants leg was ripped all the way down to the ankle. Then I saw the hole in my flesh and asked for a handkerchief, impatient to get back to that cow.

"No, no, you're not going back," Alejandro said.

I gave him a look of scorn and started for the cow. I

wasn't going to let a *puntazo* (puncture) keep me from finishing.

"But, *hombre*, you have a *cornada* [horn wound]," Alejandro said, looking worried.

"Good," I said. "Maybe now I can catch up on a little sleep."

Most sympathetically, Montani offered to carry me out.

"I can walk," I said, waving him away.

"No, *señorita*, we're going out." He swept me off my feet and carried me through the narrow exits. Three others helped him carry me all the way to the house. I kept looking back.

"How many cows left?" I said.

"None."

I repeated the question, and was again assured that there were no others to be tested that day. I had known that, but it didn't seem to register.

"*En hora buena para ella* [a good hour for her]," I said referring to that last cow with the term of congratulation given a successful matador after a *corrida*.

Then I tried to excuse myself for having fought badly and for being such a trouble. I wanted to know where Alejandro was. Someone said he was coming.

"He was anything but pleased with me," I said.

"How could he be displeased after what happened?" Montani questioned, just as Alejandro caught up with us.

I asked him if it were not true and Alejandro grunted.

"You see?" I said to Montani.

Then I noticed how serious everyone looked, so I

laughed and hummed the Chopin "Funeral March." They didn't seem amused. Then I began to think, so this is what a goring is. I tried to put all my thinking into my leg, but I kept noticing that it was twilight and the birds were still chirping in the trees along the lane. I kept trying to think how it felt, and all I could decide was that it was like a bee sting. They took me into a room and put me on a bed. I thought, perhaps Manolete slept here. The *señora*, Don Pepe's wife came in, and they looked at the leg. I didn't want to look at it. I just kept thinking, so this is a goring.

Then I thought of a Joel McCrae motion picture I had seen in which he rides to a ranch with a wounded arm. Of course there was a beautiful girl at the ranch house to receive him. In spite of her protests he poured powder from revolver shells into the wound and lit it with a match. The explosion cauterized the wound and stopped the bleeding. That's bravery, I thought, something that has always fascinated me. This would be a grand time to show my fortitude by suggesting that they stop the bleeding as Joel McCrae had done in the movie. I thought that was what they had been trying to do. I hadn't realized yet that Montani was probing around, trying to find out how far in the horn had gone and how many trajectories there were. He suddenly touched something that really hurt, and I decided not to do a Joel McCrae just then. I must have been half-gone; I can't remember all he did. I know he had to cut off the pants leg and that he said something about my not minding, since I wouldn't want to wear them again anyway as they were not only torn but soaked with blood. He did

158

all the cleansing, and I guess Alejandro helped him with the bandage.

When he was through, Montani gave me a pill and told me to take it with a glass of water. As though he hadn't heard my refusal, he took it back and stuffed it down my throat. I had wanted to go through it without a pill, to help make up for my poor showing. Besides, I had thought that I would scorn gorings. I did try to laugh it off. I joked about it.

"Patricia," Don Pepe said, "you know the life of a bullfighter is *cornadas y dinero* [gorings and money]."

I smiled politely. I really think I was proud that I'd been gored.

Montani wrapped me in a blanket and carried me to the car. He propped me up with pillows and we drove slowly to town. I thought that there were things I had to remember before it was too late, things I would have to practice most. Here they are, just as I wrote them in the car:

"*Mover—exercises para fuerza en los pies, pitón a pitón, tirón a tirón, tanteo*—14 de Enero, 1953—Santa Macarena. (Movements—exercises for strength in the feet, horn-to-horn passes [flapping lower end of *muleta* at the bull's muzzle and jerking it back or to the side to draw bull out of place where he has chosen to stand], passes to see how bull charges—14 of January, 1953—Holy Macarena.)

"Make the cross or the devil gets you (as they say of going in to kill. If you don't cross your *muleta* over to the right under your sword, you can't lead the bull that way so you can get out from the horns.).

"Fight bull to his capacity. The shame is a great bull and a matador who is afraid or doesn't give him a good fight. Bravery is in the bull. I don't think of bravery. Make the bull come around to your way of fighting.

"*Orfebres* [artists] as opposed to *dominadores* [dominators]—Dominguin, Arruza, examples of latter. Pepe Ortiz and Alejandro, examples of former.

"Three things make a bullfighter immortal:

1. *Alegria* (gaiety in the ring and variety, as opposed to serious domination with limited repertoire).

2. *Temple* (the slowness with which the passes are made).

3. *Salero* (literally, salty, but spice is meant, personality).

"These leave eternal memory in minds of *aficionados* and give men 'category.' "

When we arrived at Dr. Duque's, I cried from embarrassment rather than from pain. Now I felt ashamed. So they laughed, said it was just a *puntaza*. Dr. Duque kidded me, but he got me on the operating table before I knew what was up, without even taking off the rest of my pants. He operated for an hour without giving me any anesthetic. I just gripped a handkerchief of Dad's I'd carried, and I swore I wouldn't yell. I asked the doctor if he didn't think Montani had put on a good bandage. Dr. Duque took it off and cleaned the wound with ether. He had to cut the hole larger to get into the wound.

I found myself making terrific noises against my will. I just couldn't hold them back any more; they just came, as though from another. I didn't want to for more than my sake—not to disturb anyone, as well as so they couldn't say that I couldn't take it. Alejandro held my legs down. *Señora* Duque sometimes hugged me to her. She begged me to cry, but I just couldn't, not because I was brave but because I was dried up or didn't know how. I can't analyze it; crying with me is more from fear or frustration.

I have accepted pain since I was a child, but only to tolerate it. Once I ate too many green apples and got a stomach ache, but it went away. I always hated the idea of discipline by pain. As a child I had to be spanked three times a week. I often wondered about the use of pain to govern people. Fear I could understand, but pain was still a curiosity and so now I tried to study this pain; but it was like someone talking too much— only I couldn't walk out on this.

I remembered Hemingway refusing anesthetic in the Spanish Civil War because it was scarce and the men needed it. An American among brave Latins, showing he could be brave too. I wanted to be brave, but the pain came in cycles, such pain as I had not known possible. I learned the cycle and to wait for the pain that swelled beyond control. I tried to measure it and see if I couldn't hold out against it longer each time. And then I waited for it to go down again. I thought that if I could sing I might hold back the screams that came involuntarily from my throat. I remembered how a teacher had said that I couldn't be a great singer because I couldn't control my diaphragm and was too throaty. I thought, well now I can try it. I started to sing a Spanish song:

Los Piconeros

"Ay, que me diga que sí
Ay, que me diga que no,
Cómo no lo ha querío
Ninguno lo quiero yo
Mi piconero, como el picón
Por tu curpa
Curpita, yo tengo
Negro, negrito
Mi corozón!"

It was pretty throaty and didn't all come at once. Dr.
Duque said I sang it for Montani's benefit.

They put me in a room adjoining the operating room.
The lovely *señora* brought me tea. The men went to the
Fausto Restaurant after assuring me the wound was
only a *puntaza,* and that I would be able to fight the
next Sunday. Consuelo, the sister of Rafael Rodriguez,
the famous matador, came and talked to me. She spoke
of the agony the sister and mother of a bullfighter go
through each time they know he is fighting. She said she
never went to see her brother in the ring. (He's still
fighting.)

"Cornadas y dinero." I tried to sound chipper imitat-
ing Don Pepe.

Señora Duque brought a replica of the Virgin of San
Juan and placed it over the head of my bed.

Other visitors came in the evening. The first was Alfonso Ramirez, Calisero, with whom I'd fought my first
tienta and who had vouched for me with the union, bless
his heart. He had suffered one of the worst gorings: six

trajectories inside the main goring, from being tossed around on the horn. One of them had hit the femoral artery.

"Now you've had your baptism of blood," he said, and, to me, it was like a congratulation or a benediction. I felt that now I was really in the fraternity of matadors.

Don Bilbao of Juárez came, and others. Montani came to see how I was and to say good-by, as he had to leave Aguascalientes for a fight somewhere. He was very gentle and tried to be most helpful, as though he hadn't already done much.

"Bullfighting is like arithmetic," he said. "Two plus two equals four. If it doesn't, there's a mistake and we have to correct it."

"There are three ways of getting gored," he continued a little later, "First, error, wrong judgment. Second, a bad pass, one made badly. Third, a freak accident, where the wind blows the cape or the bull raises his head for no good reason—like when Jesús Córdoba had his face split open."

I turned away. There was no use asking which mistake I'd made, with the example of arithmetic to make clear what he meant. I don't remember what else he said. He sat by the bed for a while and talked. But what he had said made me pensive. I remember the flashing of his eyes and his seriousness and great courtesy. I made up my mind that I liked him, in spite of the "matadora" incident.

"Don't worry about this afternoon," he said very slowly. "You fought very well."

"*Gracias*, matador," was all I could say.

People started teasing me about him. "How does it

feel to be carried in by a handsome matador?" I was asked that first night.

I counted the hours and minutes that night; the leg was pretty painful for about forty-eight hours. I was never so glad to see the morning. But all during the days I had visitors in and out. And such visitors! Matadors, priests, girls, and even a cockfight man who talked to me of that.

Rafael Rodriguez was a great tease. He later brought his lovely fiancée to see me. He told me to keep a pillow under my leg to ease the pain, and he said that what he hated the most about gorings was the bedpan. Luís Procuna said he would just as soon go without the ether as smell it, and he and Pepe Luís asked me if I noticed that it sounded like cutting rubber when they pared away the flesh to clean and probe the wound. I said I didn't know because I had thought they were sewing it up, but they hadn't closed it at first—that didn't come until Friday when Dr. Duque operated again, with anesthetic. Armillita (who had had only one goring during his long career and who had seen that one coming but had taken it, rather than give ground when he couldn't defend himself) asked me for an autographed photograph. It was one of the nicest compliments I've ever had. He had it framed and it hangs in his ranch house.

Other matadors who called while I was recuperating included Humberto Moro, Juan Espinosa, and Ricardo Balderas. All talked of gorings, usually as though in jest. All agreed that the most painful part of any is the treatment. On Sunday, after church, children came with candy and ice cream for me.

On Thursday, after being carried to the office, I had

telephoned my parents. They had already read about it
in the papers. I told them not to pay any attention, that
it was just a *puntaza*. Mother was much upset and
wanted to come down. It was a bad connection. I told
her to listen carefully. I said that I had walked to the
phone—lie number one. I repeated that I was okay, and
that I was up and walking around, since it was only a
puntaza—lie number two. I really did think it was a
puntaza, at first. I read in the papers the day after the
goring that it was twenty-five centimeters deep (about
nine inches). I was told that that was just publicity and
newspaper talk. When I wanted to get up three days
later I found out that the papers had been right. I wasn't
even allowed to take a bath.

Señora Chebela Duque baked a cake for me and
brought it in with one candle on it on January 20, my
first anniversary. I still have the candle. I served cake
to everyone who came in the evening. The next day I took
my first steps. I was all right, not too dizzy. I didn't need
the cane, but I saved that for when I went out—a bullfighter with a goring! I even practiced how I would use
it. Hammy!

I thought I could bathe for the visit of the Garfias
family, but no luck. I had to take things slowly. Dr.
Duque gave me a book on the life of Belmonte to keep
me quiet, though I walked a little more each day. I
stayed in the sun. I had a diet of ham and chicken and
green salad and milk. The doctor and Chebela were
wonderful!

I had read in the bullfight papers that now it could
be decided whether or not I would become a bullfighter.
They say one cannot tell until after a goring how well

one will face the bulls. The effects of fear! I wondered about this. When Alejandro returned from a fight in Leon, I asked him about all the speculation in the papers about how I'd fight.

"Don't worry about it," he said. "The only ones who are too frightened are the ones who don't know how to fight."

About ten days after the goring I tried practicing in the Aguascalientes ring, and on the twenty-ninth I went to a *tienta* at Penuelas, another of the famous *ganaderías*. I had been invited but was doubly honored when Armillita, who couldn't attend, asked me to represent him at the *tienta*. Calisero Luis Procuna, Ricardo Balderas, Pepe Luís Vasquez, and Humberto Moro were also at Penuelas. I fought six cows. It was wonderful; free of bed and bedpan, though the wound was still draining, I could bathe again. I'd had my punishment and was glad to be back at play—and work—again. I can forget pain. And I know that the bull too is not dominated by pain, and so I respect him.

I fought with both cape and *muleta*. When a cow got difficult and Luís Procuna came in to take her away, I shouted "*Déjala!*" asking them to leave her alone and get out. I felt that I did all right.

Papers in the States quoted me as saying that I'd be glad to take revenge on that cow. I made no such statements. Revenge is not taken out on an animal, but by correcting one's own faults. I wanted to do this with the *muleta* and I did. Revenge, in the sense in which the papers mentioned it, is taken only after a matador is gored or killed in the ring, when another matador goes in to kill the bull for the fallen one.

I went to Acapulco with Alejandro, who was to fight in the *cuadrilla* of Jesús Córdoba on a program with Montani and Caesar Gijon. I wasn't sure I wanted to see that fight, for if Montani didn't measure up as a bull-fighter to what he seemed to be as a person, I'd have been disappointed. Not that I had romantic ideas about him; that was out of the question for me since I'd chosen to become a matadora. But I enjoyed the trip, through Cuernavaca and tropical country. We arrived the night before the fight. I had a room in a house, while the *cuadrilla* went to a motel. After Alejandro thought me safely deposited for the night, I went out and walked along the seashore. I had the whole beach to myself. I took off my shoes. It was perfect, the wind in my face and the cold water lapping at my feet.

The next morning a correspondent asked me about my goring and I denied that it had been painful.

"Ha, ha!" said Jesús Córdoba. "I know they are painful."

"Yes, but I have more padding." I said.

I saw Montani coming out of the church. He waved and came over to talk with us and went through the formalities of asking how I was feeling. He seemed to be in a hurry and soon went off with Gijon.

I saw the fight. Montani's bull was bad and he didn't cut anything, but he did well, especially with *chicueli-nas*. Those were the biggest bulls I had seen—over five years old. Montani received a *puntaza* in the right thigh, just below a former goring. I knew it would be the last time I'd see him and it was. I never saw him after he left the ring. He cut his *coleta* (pigtail, emblem of the *torero*) on Easter, retiring from the ring, and went back to Peru.

The next day we went deep-sea fishing with Córdoba, Antonio Ordonez, Pancho Balderas, and a Madrid correspondent who had come to Mexico with Dominguin. I got a strike as soon as I sat down and was strapped to the seat—after much careful explanation. It was a fair-sized, adult sailfish. The Madrid newsman had sat for two hours without a nibble. Jesús Córdoba got the biggest of the day. I enjoyed it so much that Alejandro said that if I weren't a bullfighter I'd probably become a sailor. I had been fishing in the Gulf of Mexico out of New Orleans when a child, so it wasn't really my first time at sea!

We picked up José Padilla in Mexico City on the way to San Miguel de Allende and the Pepe Ortiz *tienta*. Padilla had once been the valet of Ortiz and is now one of the best tailors in Mexico. (He makes my bullfighting clothes.) He told me on the trip that San Miguel was one place in Mexico that I wouldn't like; that there was no romance there such as I'd found in Aguascalientes and San Luis Potosí; that they didn't even have electricity, and that I'd have to bathe out of a pitcher. After we had turned off the highway onto a dusty road, about four hours out of Mexico City, he pointed out one dusty village after another and said, "See what they are like out this way." I'd ask at each village if it was San Miguel. Finally, at a good-sized town, Padilla said it was not San Miguel, but Santa Rosa, the sweetheart of San Miguel, meaning that we were getting warmer. And a few minutes later we were entering San Miguel.

We climbed up the side of a hill which had lovely, balconied houses built on the slope. Below a great valley spread out. We passed the beautiful home of Cantinflas, the great Mexican actor, and then that of Pepe Ortiz, and dropped down into the town, with its cathedral and old palaces built around the plaza. It was spectacular, the antithesis of all that Padilla had told me. I found that it is a center of art; a place where celebrities live when they retire, and I don't wonder, it is such a beautiful place.

We went to the Hotel San Francisco which seemed more a palace than a commercial inn. Of course there was electricity, too, and conveniences. I was really taken aback after all the kidding on the trip.

Pepe Ortiz and some other gentlemen were in the lobby when we arrived. I was so stunned by the beauty of the entrance patio, and the surroundings in general, that it was almost too much to find this man, with the kindest eyes I've ever seen, swarthy skin and white hair and gentle manner, greeting us.

"Es bonita," he said to the person who introduced us. (She's pretty.)

I could have said how long I'd wanted to meet him and how thrilled I was, but I was probably awkward with joy and embarrassment and the lovely surroundings.

We ate while my room was being arranged. Alejandro and Padilla had to go to another hotel. I thought that if I ever have a ranch the rooms will be like the one I had, simple but large and somehow magnificent. Fine, plain furniture, and on the wall just a simple cross over the bed. I was meditative for a long time before going to sleep.

I was up bright and early and found Pepe already in the lobby. He asked me to have breakfast with him, and I almost disobeyed my maestro and accepted. He probably wouldn't have objected to my accepting the invitation from Ortiz, but it was an iron rule that I wait for him before doing anything with anyone else. I told Pepe that I'd have to wait for my teacher. (We were scarcely on speaking terms.) Pepe called Alejandro and Padilla and in about half an hour they arrived. Ortiz explained that it had been his idea to phone; he was such a gentleman even in little ways. I bow my head to this man.

Pepe Ortiz had been first interested in the stage. There is a joke that his friend, the singer Pedro Vargas, wanted to be a bullfighter and Ortiz a singer. Ortiz had sung, he was once the toreador in the opera *Carmen*. He had a beautiful voice and the figure for it; the figure helped make him a bullfighter. He was in the ring, fighting, the day that Gaona cut his *coleta* and said farewell to professional fighting. It was the day of retirement for one great figure and the birth of another.

At one time Ortiz decided that he had to be either a priest or a bullfighter. He carried a heavy cross in the ring; had terrific gorings and perhaps more punishment from the bulls than any other figure, though it was mostly from bad luck. One goring split his tongue. But he was a tremendous artist, the greatest Mexico had, and one of the most loved of all matadors. He was in a class all by himself, as was Gaona, his idol.

He married a beautiful actress who had played Juana Inez de la Cruz in the picture of the same name. (She

170

had the flu when I was there, but I met their nine-year-old daughter.) Pepe too had acted in pictures, among others *Hora de Verdad (Hour of Truth)* about a matador. He made a couple of films with Conchita Cintron. He showed me stills of her from those pictures. A man of many talents, he also writes music, and his house is perfect in every way, reflecting his taste and his love for beauty. His parade cape hung in a glass case in the library. Whenever you see a picture of a matador looking over his shoulder with the Virgin of Guadalupe embroidered on his cape, that's Pepe Ortiz.

He gave me a pair of beautiful *banderillas* with the colors of his ranch, and a *palillo* which is still my favorite. I'll show it to my grandchildren, if I ever have any. I couldn't have been happier than at his house, after the testing. There had been lights and shadows that were interesting when I met him at the hotel, and I was again conscious of the light when at his house. I can remember it by the atmosphere and the light and shade, made dramatic by a sudden thunderstorm that dimmed and finally extinguished the lights. Then, in the quiet dark, the light on his face when he puffed at his cigar.

At his ranch they were testing young bulls. I had no part in that but I fought a few cows. I'd heard Pepe say that, with the exception of Conchita, women bullfighters were apt to be torpid, were not quick enough at certain given moments to do instinctively what had to be done. I wanted to prove otherwise and he was most generous in his praise. Respecting him as I do, I can only believe him.

But my leg was still secreting, and I certainly didn't move as well as I should have, though there was no great pain. With one cow I certainly didn't do well at keeping her in the right terrain. "Let me at her again," I said, and they all laughed.

Pepe explained that my slowness in *reponer* was due to my leg. I fought this cow again. I swear she knew I was a woman. She'd run off across the ring and wait for me, trying to wear me out chasing her. I got so hot I could taste my own blood, but it was me or her even if I got another goring. Finally I could hardly hold up the *muleta*—and she just played with me. As soon as the boys got in with her, she fought well!

I fought again the next day and did better. I wore Spanish boots Rafael had given me when I was at Dr. Duque's. They are the kind that fold just right at the ankle and yet support the legs a little. I was getting stronger, and some of my confidence returned.

I was to fight at Reynosa in February, and without Alejandro, who was ordered to fight in Mexico City in honor of the Virgin of Guadalupe on the same Sunday. I was a little worried about this, since it would be the first *corrida* since my goring, though Mariano Rivera would take Alejandro's place as *de brega* (the *banderillero* who advises the matador—"the confidential peon," he is sometimes called). Of course Martín, my sword handler and companion at *corrida* towns, went with me on the two-day bus trip. We enjoyed it and had our fill of *cabrito* (kid), which we eat morning, noon, and night when anywhere near Monterrey. Then bad weather caused the *corrida* to be postponed and we went back to Juárez.

We were back again in Reynosa March 1, and this time the *corrida* was held. The judges granted me an ear but Alejandro wouldn't let me accept it. He wasn't pleased with my fight, though I thought that the wind was a far worse enemy than the bull. I did not feel the fear it had been said might make me give ground, but the wind made it very hard to control the cape, though Martín wet it and rubbed sand in it to make it heavier.

When the Señora Duque had hung the beautiful Virgin of San Juan de Los Lagos over my bed, I had vowed to go to Her basilica in San Juan, Jalisco, and give Her my first ear cut that year, if I was cured soon enough to go on *tientas*. I wanted to cut ears for Her on the first fight. Alejandro said that when I cut ears for Her I would have to earn them better than I had the first one.

I cut the next ear, one that Alejandro let me accept, on Easter Day, though that *corrida* should also have been suspended on account of the wind. I did what I could and fought as well as I could, but the wind kept exposing me and I was hooked a couple of times and knocked down when the cape blew away and left me alone for target. Those were the largest bulls I had fought to that time (400 kilos). I was sorry about the wind, but Alejandro said I fought to his satisfaction.

On May 3, I cut four ears and one tail and felt I was really back in the running. This was at my old favorite, Villa Acuña. I got two ears and a tail the next fight in May, at Nogales, though I was thrown and stepped on. I wasn't as worried about the trampling as by that bull's teeth; the critter wanted to bite. He had a fine set of molars and seemed to enjoy using them.

Hoof and mouth disease called off the *corrida* I was to have in Nuevo Laredo, but on the fourth of July I cut ears and a tail at Reynosa, and two ears and a tail the following day back at Villa Acuña. I was looking forward to a fight at Tijuana, and wanted to cut something right through that fight in the big ring there.

One dream I have is to hit the road and fight regularly like many top matadors who barely have time to get from one *corrida* to another. I seemed to have more zest since the goring. I certainly felt that I was learning; and I thought, the thicker they come, the better. I had lost no part of my ambition with the blood-letting at the *tienta* and felt more confident than ever since my "baptism."

Tijuana was important to me. There are large crowds from California which attend, and the La Punta bulls I'd been promised were an added lure. We arrived at Tijuana three days before the *corrida*, and I practiced in the big ring. Alejandro was annoyed with me, and I got whacked with the sword a couple of times. We had planned to go to Los Angeles for a television show, but found that we couldn't because of passport difficulties.

The city was crowded when I left the hotel for the ring. We went early because of the traffic. I was dressed as usual, except that I was wearing Spanish leather chaps over the *campero* pants. We arrived at the ring half an hour early and I had to sign autographs until I thought my arm would drop off. The arena seemed full —over 11,000 people. When I bowed to the judges after the parade into the ring, I noticed movie stars in the front shady seats. I felt that it was going to be a big day.

The second *novillero* was gored under the armpit by the second bull, but he stayed and killed him before being taken to the infirmary. I was to have the third and last bulls of the afternoon, the only ones from La Punta.

I watched my first bull charge into the ring. He was fast and seemed to follow the trailing cape when Alejandro ran him. I did all right with *veronicas* and heard applause and music, but with the *rebolero* with which I finished them he floored me. I couldn't figure out why; I thought I had done it properly, and I was told it was a beauty.

When Pancho Balderas came to the barrier after planting *banderillas*, he told me to be careful, that the bull was not to be trusted. So I did not dedicate him when I went out for the *faena*.

When I doubled him I noticed that he passed well on one side but was uncertain on the other. I discovered that he took the left-hand passes well and wanted to fight. I encouraged him with a high pass and he went through perfectly. Then I cited him for *derechazos* (right-hand passes), and he passed all right on the first. There was a little wind, but not as bad as I'd had before that year. I cited him for another right-hand pass and he charged straight for me instead of the *muleta*. I fixed it, but he didn't see the *muleta* at all. I knew he was going to get me when I couldn't get his attention off me, but I wouldn't run. He took me, all right. As he tossed me and, as I fell over his horn, it caught in my high boot. I felt the familiar bee sting a couple of times before I got loose and hit the ground. As soon as he was taken away I grabbed the sword and *muleta* and went after him. I felt a strange stiffness in my leg, but I thought it would wear off. Then I got woozy in the head and could hardly stand. Someone started to take me out, but I came to my senses and protested. I had to kill that bull.

That was all that was in my head—that my bull be dead before I left the ring.

I was ordered from the ring four times by the judges. I had to kick and punch the men and policeman trying to carry me until they let go. Then I proved to myself, too late, that the bull was blind in one eye. I finally killed that bull, though. It took two short thrusts (his head was still high) and a half thrust. And I gave him the *descabello*.

Then I limped over to the front of the judges' stand and received an ear. Gilbert Roland, who was seated in the front row beneath the judges, threw his hat into the ring. I blew him a kiss and walked around the ring under my own power. I think everyone was standing up. Someone even took off his shoes and tossed them down. I've never heard such a roar as that crowd made. Before I finished the circuit, the blood was running out over the top of my boot, and I started worrying about my next bull, which had been considered the better of my two. But I soon learned that I was not to return from the operating table to the ring. That worried me the most.

He had tossed me again after getting his horn thirteen inches into the calf of my leg, and had made a trajectory of nine inches off the main wound. It was peculiar; the wound was from the top of the calf, right under my knee, down toward the ankle. It is possible that I would not have been gored had not my boot caught on the horn and held my leg there as I went over his head. It had also torn the muscles badly, which had made it so painful to walk. When they started probing, I sang arias from the Spanish opera *La Dolorosa* to keep from thinking about it, but I must have yelled anyway. Alejandro was sitting on my back. This was painful because of the torn muscles, but not much of a counterirritant when they started cutting the wound clean and pouring ether into it.

"What do you think, that there's a meat shortage?" I remember asking as they operated.

Then I guess I went out of my head, for I kept moaning about losing that second bull. I was put in an ambulance and taken to a hospital, while my friend Joselito Mendez won acclaim with my second La Punta bull.

Nine

The Jealous Virgins

I was not clear-headed, of course; there was the shock and the disappointment in not being able to finish the *corrida;* but I felt that I had erred in some way that did not involve my training in the art of bull-fighting. There was luck, but is luck just chance? I'm not so sure. That afternoon on the way to the hospital from the Tijuana ring, I thought perhaps my error had been a neglect of vows and determinations that I had made so much a part of my will that they were true, for me at least.

What troubled me most was that, though I'd promised the Virgin of Guadalupe that I would be Her sword, I had also vowed to place flowers at the feet of the Virgin del Carmen whenever I possibly could, before and after a *corrida*. I had not found Carmen in Tijuana, so I had put the flowers for Her before the Sacred Heart, and, as always, made my prayers through Fátima, my special patron to whom I'd vowed service as a matadora.

I had chosen Fátima as a special patron after reading about Her. I vowed to remember Her and what She had told the children. I promised to help her, through bullfighting, if she helped me to become a matadora. And I am most fearful of her; I usually think of and kneel to her regardless of which Virgin is represented. But I felt that it was the del Carmen whom I had slighted before this Tijuana fight. I couldn't put it from my mind.

Gilbert Roland, the actor and *aficionado*, was allowed to come to the hospital room after the fight. He was most cordial and sympathetic. I was still a little dizzy, to say the least, but I realized that I was honored by the visit of such a celebrity who also knows what is what about the bulls. I told him about my thoughts.

"Could they be jealous?" I tried to be less serious.

Gilbert immediately removed his own medal of Fátima, which he said he carried always, and insisted that I keep it with me in the hospital. He did not seem to think my woozy talk strange, for he said he understood how I felt about Carmen.

I don't pretend to understand these things; I go only by intuition. I have been laughed at because I have vows to so many Virgins. But to me each is real, and each has her place in the mystical part of my make-up. All this is involved somehow with that which makes me a bullfighter, though that too is hard for many to understand. There is a deep relationship between the Brave Festival and the spiritual. Religion overlaps both, in more ways than in ceremony and ritual. Some of the greatest matadors admit to the mystical element in bull-fighting, though they cannot reason it out much better than I can. But who can reason the mysteries of religion? Are they not both beyond reason?

I have always been religious, though I used to fall asleep sitting in a church. But God is and always has been a great mystery—and not in a superstitious way (though I respect superstitions). I can think of no greater mystery than the life of Christ. I remember, as a child, the first great mystery of my life was the Man on the cross. Why had it been necessary that He should suffer? It made a deep impression on me. I don't think it was compassion I felt. It was startling and shocking. A mystery I couldn't unravel. But it was so impressed on me that He was good, and that it had been for others, that I accepted it as good and necessary even though I could not understand it.

Mother was a member of the Altar Guild of the Epis-copal Church. Sometimes I would go with her while she attended her duties in the sanctuary. It was impressed on me that I should not go to the altar until I was con-firmed. So there was something mysterious there too. And there were the stained-glass windows which showed the wounded hands and feet. And the dim atmosphere, the shadows.

This was the one mystery the meaning of which I wanted to discover that went along with the mystery I felt in that first bullfight and my inexplainable desire to become a matador. Perhaps it was a desire to know, the old fixation of mine for discovery, which usually meant finding the meaning. I do not think it actually had much to do with suffering, though there was that too.

I hear people talk of the nobility of suffering in connection with fighting. But I don't hold with any idea like that in the ring. Every woman probably goes through a Joan of Arc period, and men too often have some idea of its nobility. The nobility of matadors is not of suffering. The basis of bullfighting is not being hurt by the bull, any more than it is hurting the bull for the pleasure of hurting. Actually, it is questionable if the bull suffers at all in the heat of his short fight, doing what he would rather do than anything else.

And it is not so that I won't suffer that I pray, even before a fight. It is my responsibility to see that I defend myself with what art and skill I can, with cape and *muleta*. And it is not fear that causes me to pray. It is that I may do my best not only for those who have paid to see me but for my own satisfaction; that I may do justice to the bull, and make of the festival as far as I can what it is meant to be. And most of all it is to discover the secret in it. I go to the chapel because the feelings I have are too big for me, and I realize that there is more to it than just the physical thing that seems to be me.

The Virgins were all women, naturally, and somehow seem more approachable by a woman, though the men pray too before their fights and make vows and journeys to repay vows. God, being infinite, may be reached more easily by a humble soul who does not know how to communicate with Him, if He is sought through the mediation of these saints. So I have prayed to many Virgins since seeking my career in Mexico.

La Macarena is the general patron Virgin of all bull-fighters, Spanish or Latin American. Guadalupe is the patron of Mexico and therefore of Mexican fighters. Every chapel in every plaza in Mexico has Guadalupe and usually also a smaller Macarena.

On my first visit to Mexico City as a bullfighter, I went to the cathedral and made my great vow to Guadalupe, the most important vow of all, and one that I cannot disclose until I retire from the ring or the day of my death. It is really more than a vow, and it must be completed on my part; it is not just a favor to be handed me gratis.

When I first went to Aguascalientes for *tientas* I went to the church of San Marcos. There is the Virgin of Carmen. One is invited to make three wishes before her, and of course mine all pertained to bullfighting. I remember Her whenever I think of those wishes, and whenever I am to fight I take flowers to Her.

At Dr. Duque's, I prayed to the Virgin of San Juan of the Lakes. I still have the first ear I cut (that my maestro would let me keep) wrapped up to take to her basilica when I am near enough to Jalisco to make the journey.

There are numerous Virgins in Mexico, each with her particular legend and her devotees. But Fátima is the one I asked to be my special patron, because her story appealed to me and I found her picture in the Juárez Chapel when, emotional and earnest, I first went into it with my great wish to become what then seemed impossible, a matadora.

So I was very happy to have the medal Gilbert Roland left with me after my Tijuana goring. I still wondered if I would have discovered sooner that my bull was blind if I had been more faithful to del Carmen before the fight. For I am still convinced that the reason that bull caught me was that I was all he could see. No matter how I fixed the *muleta* with my right hand, he could not see it on that side. When I got up after the goring, I proved that he was blind in his left eye. I knew I would have to try to kill him quickly, since it would be impossible to fight him well under such conditions. And I knew I would have a hard time doing that, even if I had two good legs, since I had to go over the horn above his good eye. I gave him high and horn-to-horn passes, in spite of my leg, to prepare him. Crossing the *muleta* to turn his head to the left was of little use if his vision was all on the side where I had to be. It may not have been "pretty" fighting, but it was all that could be done under the circumstances.

It is for guidance from such unforeseen situations that I pray that the Virgin will be with me during my fight.

Gilbert Roland came down from Hollywood to visit me again on the Thursday after the fight. He brought a new medal of Fátima for me to keep and a case with pictures of the Virgin Mary and Christ to take with me on my travels. I open this handsome case on my dresser before each fight now and light a candle before it. The case is similar to one that Manolete always carried, Gilbert said.

Gilbert Roland brought other gifts, and he made a gay time of his visit for the convalescent. He insisted that what a bullfighter needs to recover his strength after a goring is Spanish omelette, or *tortilla*, and immediately went out and had one made and brought it to me. It was good; I liked it. I have had other wonderful gifts from Mr. Roland, and his encouragement and interest have meant much. He even got permission to take me to a *corrida* two weeks after I was gored, and I sat on a pillow beside him where he had been during the *corrida* in which I fought.

I can skip over most of the period in the hospital. I missed my friends of my former convalescence and the good Duques. There were visitors, of course, but it was hardly the atmosphere of Dr. and Señora Duque's home or the atmosphere of bullfighting that lingers always over Aguascalientes.

I'll never forget one incident at the clinic in Tijuana. Most bullfighters agree that the treatments are far more painful than the goring, but this doctor told me that his fingers were so sensitive (the most sensitive in his field among medical men) that he could detect pain before his patient felt it, and therefore, he said, he was one of the most painless doctors practicing. All the time he was telling me this he was probing around my sore leg with fingers that felt like cold steel, while with the other hand he carried chocolate (I always had it on hand for visitors—and myself) to his mouth and crunched it while he spoke.

I tried to think of something funny to keep from showing the pain he "couldn't" inflict. I didn't tell him, but it occurred to me that if his ancestors had been on the Spanish Armada, and mine had helped to sink it, a little Spanish revenge was being dealt out in typically Spanish fashion—quietly and diplomatically. The upper half of me was practically shimmying up and down the ironwork at the head of the bed while I tried to agree with him sweetly and control the automatic reactions to the electriclike shocks he was sending up my body. I had to "be brave" and tell him only when it "really" hurt.

That type of wound is slow to heal, and it had to be cleaned constantly. When finally I was allowed to try standing on it, I found that I couldn't straighten my knee or bend my foot at the ankle. It was as though my leg had stiffened into the position a ballet dancer holds when she is on her toes. When I could walk a few steps, it still remained stiff and unbendable. Pedro Calderon and another picador used to push against my toes while I'd try to push my heel against them to bend my foot to a more normal position. I even had to get used to sitting up in a chair, for when my foot was down, the blood going to it made it throb painfully. But I was relieved to be assured that it would eventually return to normal, and that it would not be likely to interfere with fighting dates.

I returned to Juárez on the fifteenth day after the goring and went straight to Dr. Acuña. He gave me penicillin and ordered me to stay in bed for three days. The first day in bed I got so restless that I sneaked out of the house and walked almost two blocks. The wound healed more rapidly, and in another two weeks I was able to start practicing, a little more each day. Soon I could feel the stiffness only when I first started to practice; then it would loosen up and I could forget it.

When I can't practice, I always become restless. And then I find it hard to sleep, even at night. Twilight and late evening are always a bad time for me to try to sleep, and this is worse during enforced inactivity. It is a mystic time, and sometimes it makes me morbid with the old and lonely feelings. I don't mean that I consider myself lonely, but there is certainly that in each of us that cannot be shared. And after all, I am a foreigner whose own country is not in sympathy with what I believe in and with what I am trying to do. And of course I cannot, and don't wish to, be other than what I am, a North American girl. I have little sympathy for those of us who go to Mexico and attempt to be more Mexican than those born in the country and of a different heritage. That is not what I am trying to do at all. But because I am what I am, I am sometimes lonely, even with people. It is just that I have different values from those usual among my compatriots north of the Border. It has nothing to do with whether they are better or lesser values.

It is as José Maria Cossio says of bullfighting, that it must be understood to have a deep meaning in the way of life of Spanish peoples, so that politics, industry and artistic pursuits all have traces of it, no matter how bullfighting may be judged from moral or sentimental points of view. It is a fact which no judgment can eliminate. Whether we like another's values or not has little bearing on their realities. Integrity—what I always call the truth—is what seems most important to me; and the way I get at that in myself is what makes me do what I do.

I do a lot of thinking, or meditating, on these things before going to sleep. Often, I admit, it seems a little morbid. If my exhaustion permits me to fall asleep quickly, there is still that moment between consciousness and the forgetfulness that is sound sleep when my mind wanders over thoughts of what life is for and what death is. I sometimes think that if I could sleep (and how sweet that desire sometimes is) it would be like death—not even to know existence or nonexistence. I wonder, then, if punishment for sins might not be such total darkness—not even a memory of what we had felt and experienced while living, a life that would end and mean nothing. That might be hell, to have life blotted out as though worthless. Life is no sweeter to a bullfighter than to anyone else, but he wants to accomplish what he lives for and find meaning in his life. Then I think that to do that he must do all in his power to become a better bullfighter, and the possibility of sleep becomes more remote than ever as I go over the things I must learn by hard work, since I'm not a genius.

There is an old Spanish saying that I've heard. I can't remember just how it goes, but it is something like this: If the life of a bullfighter has been completely dedicated to his art, then, if the bull takes his life, his heart is ready to be received by God for what it is.

I am not afraid of death; it is a mystery and perhaps the greatest adventure of all. From the earliest times of man as a conscious being, it has fascinated him, and it frequently has been connected with the bulls and with religion. The bull always has been a symbol of mysterious force and courage. Traces of this regard for the bull are found in the remains of many primitive cultures.

To the ancient Egyptians a white bull (sometimes with the body of a man) was the symbol of the soul of Osiris or the reincarnation of the father of all the gods. Bulls were used, and sometimes fought, in the religious rituals. And women performed, so we can say that there have always been women bullfighters. It is simply that none of them starred as the men did, until Juanita Cruz and later, Conchita Cintron.

Three thousand years ago bulls were used in religious ceremonies in Crete; and the Greeks at one time, under the domination of Minos, king of Crete, were forced to pay as tribute a yearly shipment of seven youths and seven maidens to be sacrificed to the Minotaur. Theseus was probably the first fighter in history to volunteer to fight a bull to death when he volunteered to be one of the youths. He finally killed the monster.

Mithra, the ancient Persian god of light, was represented as a young man plunging a sword into the neck of a bull, and in the rites celebrated in his honor, bulls were fought—the bull being the symbol of blind, evil force and the fighter representing good and light. In other cultures the bull also figured in religious ceremonies and sacrifices.

I remember listening to Don Felipe, a brother-in-law of Juan Belmonte, the great Spanish matador who, though twisted in body, became one of Spain's all-time greats. Felipe is interested in history and art, and he was talking about the Indians of Mexico. He does not think they came to this continent from the Orient but across an ancient land bridge between what are now the eastward bulge of South America and the westward projection of Africa. He thinks the Indians derive from Egyptians, and he cites the pyramids found in Mexico, which were built by the early inhabitants, as a proof of relationship. He believes they first built their American civilization in Peru and moved up through Central America. The sun was always their main god.

I asked Felipe about the blood sacrifices of those early Mexicans of pre-Spanish days. He said that their sun god was a warrior who came up every morning, conquered the darkness, dried the land, and made things live and grow. But even a god needed something, and for gratitude for all that he did, the Aztecs wanted to offer the highest thing in their power to give to him. It is easy to see how they felt that the life which the sun gave was the most precious thing, and so human life or blood was sacrificed, blood to sustain him, a warrior god.

We were in the car going to Mexico City from San Miguel de Allende at the time, and during a lull in the conversation I thought that it was still the same in Mexico—only now the blood was offered on those sunny Sunday afternoons in the plazas where men accept the challenge. The sun always goes with bullfighting, and he's still taking sacrifices. I too have given my sacrifice, I thought, but mine was different because it was so sweet. That was shortly after my first goring.

Felipe asked me if I had seen the picture of the Indian maiden lying with her lover watching over her. I had, for it has been reproduced in pictures and statues all over Mexico. He said she should be watched over, for underneath her were three great civilizations.

I told Don Felipe how it has been one of the disappointments of my early childhood that I had not been born an Indian.

I have noticed that some reporters express shock when I say anything about blood sacrifice and religion and bullfighting in any way that relates them to each other. Yet I have heard some of those reporters advocate the use of atom bombs and excuse the tragic suffering and death of the innocent in the destroyed enemy cities. I am not taking any stand here against war that is considered just. I merely do not understand people who are so horrified over the idea of a *corrida* because they say it is cruel to the bulls, but who can justify the maiming and killing of human beings on any scale, so long as they approve of the "cause."

I know that I am not able to make what I believe sound reasonable; I know that some will be shocked when I say that what I feel is religious and mystical in a spiritual way; and I realize that I am considered by some to be a sort of barbarian who delights in inflicting torment and death on helpless animals. I have letters charging me with this, from no doubt well-meaning countrymen of mine. You simply feel it or do not feel it. I do not consider myself cruel, and I admire and almost love the bull I face in the ring if he is noble and brave and does everything in his power to remove me from his sight and the arena.

In the first place it is pretty well realized by men who have gone through combat that most wounds do not hurt until some time after they have been received. The bull does not survive his wounds long enough to have them hurt very much, it is thought. From my own experience with two gorings, I can testify that they hurt far less when received than when the doctors get at them and for a few days thereafter. A bee sting, no more. In the second place a fighting bull is doing what he was born and bred to do. A brave bull enjoys a fight; they fight among themselves for the sport of it, much as our boys box and play football and other rough contact games.

I think bullfighting is less cruel than "sportsmen" in gay coats and on fast horses harrowing a fox over the countryside. The fox is small; he doesn't enjoy it, and he probably suffers far more from fear than the bull does from anything in the ring. I think the *corrida* is no less civilized than going out in droves each hunting season to bang away at frightened deer. And in no other contest is the man so on the short end of the odds as far as size and strength are concerned, unless perhaps in tiger or elephant hunting. I honestly can have no sympathy for a brave bull—only admiration and respect.

In Tijuana I heard someone call down that he could kill the bull, that the bull had no chance, that it was all rigged against him. I wonder what he thought when I was gored and if he thought it was just a rehearsed act then? I often hear it said that bulls are maddened before a fight, or starved, or in some way or other mistreated to make them fight. These people simply do not know that every fighter wants a bull in perfect condition. If a bull is blinded with rage or otherwise maimed, he cannot follow the capes, and the best artist in the world could not defend himself or perform well. That clear sight in a bull is imperative for a good fight was proved in my own Tijuana fight.

That bullfighting is involved with religion is less easy to demonstrate, but that millions of people gain spiritual uplift from the *corrida* cannot be denied. There certainly is no rational reason for it, any more than there is for love or the greater mysteries of the church. It is because of this that I consider it an art rather than a sport. Bullfighting at its best can do for people who understand it what great art, music, or drama can do for people who understand those mediums. At its best, art conveys a subtle something that is more than the rules and technique of the craft. It is because of this something that the serious goring or death of a great matador, such as Manolete, or Joselito before him, is a national calamity in each country where bullfighting is part of the life of the people. No military hero, no public figure of the political world or the stage, is awarded such spontaneous response. When Manolete was gored to death, millions in Spain and Latin America acted as though a member of their family had suddenly been taken by death. Why? Because he had so often proved the superiority of man over blind force, had so graciously toyed with death that it had lost some of its terror for the spectators to whom he also gave vicarious self-respect. Life is a series of challenges to almost everyone; some of us don't meet the challenges in so noble a manner as a Belmonte, Joselito, or Manolete, but we see in the ring with such matadors that it can be done.

This may sound egotistical, but it isn't. I do not know enough to write a book with all the answers to all the questions about bullfighting. And I cannot explain why it should be loved by so many. Those great matadors, who might say more than I can, will not, as a rule, because it is to them a subject which cannot be rationalized. I say what I have because I am not a Latin, and because, as a newcomer expressing her thoughts, I may indicate what happens early in the career. Those who write when they retire are full of wisdom on the subject, but they may have forgotten the impressions and concerns of their own first efforts.

The basic thing is spiritual, however I look at it. All

Ten

The Hour of Truth

For those who think my life a little rigid in the seclusion demanded, I would like to reveal a discovery I have made: The world of a bullfighter comes to him. It is not even necessary to leave the house to learn what the world is made up of. The letters! Proposals of marriage, offers of all varieties, complaints, congratulations, demands for help, what have you. From all parts of the world, letters come to the bullfighter—from crackpots, *aficionados*, and the sympathetic and intelligent. In one week I received, among other letters, the following:

A young Spaniard writes that he is stranded in Brazil;

that he has had some experience as a *torero* and possesses a consuming ambition to become a matador *de toros*. If I will help him get to Mexico he will study my "school of fighting" and work for me, and when he achieves his goal, he will dedicate not only bulls, but his career to me, with eternal gratitude to me, his patron.

This sort of letter I have to take seriously, though of course I cannot comply with his request. I know too well the yearnings to become a bullfighter, and I remember the sense of frustration when an aspirant can see no way in which he may even start to achieve his ambition. Brazil may be a Latin country, but there is no bullfighting there. The young writer might just as well be in Alaska or China for all the teaching he can acquire there. And he will have no practice other than the half-in-the-dark variety such as I indulged in at home and in the school dormitory before I was fortunate enough to find a good maestro.

Next is a letter from the editor of a health magazine. ". . . You are quoted as saying that you ate meat for strength. Under separate cover I am sending you a free sample copy of the June issue of —— magazine, which tells about the champion . . . and he has not eaten meat [for] 15 years.

"Please read the whole article about ——. I know him personally and he is a very hardy individual. What makes a horse or an elephant strong? They do not eat meat, neither does a bull."

Letters such as this one, and those from people accusing me of cruelty, I do not answer. I do not wish to try to knock the chip from anyone's shoulder. I have no doubt that many of the writers are sincere in their beliefs, as I am in mine. I respect their views but don't necessarily feel called upon to subscribe to them. But such letters may be informative!

Next is a poem, which I cannot quote since it is not my property and I judge from its tone that the author might not be happy if it were printed here. But there have been praiseworthy poems sent to me, as well as some printed in papers, from the New York *Times* to that of a small prairie town.

I have a phonograph record next, and it is a *paso doble* entitled *American Toreadora*, written by Manuel Maciste. Ha! I can puff myself a bit, perhaps, to have my own *paso doble*. All the great matadors have theirs, and they often parade into a ring while the band plays it after the *Macarena*.

Next is a letter from Mallorca, in Spanish. Enclosed is a picture of a fine-looking, stone structure, entitled *Coliseo Balear*, Plaza de Toros. The gist of the letter is as follows:

"I have read in the papers about the grand triumphs you have had in the plazas of Mexico, and believe they promise a truly great career for the valiant *torera*.

"Your brilliant performances have lead me to conceive a project which I will briefly explain:

"Here in Palma de Mallorca is a Plaza de Toros of fifteen thousand capacity. This plaza is the prettiest and happiest in Spain, well constructed, etc., in 1929.

"The proprietor of this plaza died recently and his heirs wish to sell it for a hundred thousand dollars or four million pesetas.

"I think that between your many admirers there are certainly enough men of much capital, who would con-

197

sider a disposition on your part to realize sufficient capital to buy it."

The writer goes on to say how many tourists of my dear country visit Spain, and especially Mallorca, who enjoy and applaud bullfighting. He thinks there must be many *aficionados* in North America who somehow would make my purchase, or the purchase for me by my millionaire friends, profitable. And in Mallorca there are people good at arranging *corridas*. And the *ganaderías* from which they buy bulls in Andalusia are the best in the world. The writer would be very happy to arrange everything for me.

This is by far the grandest property I have been offered to date, but my many admirers of much capital are slow in presenting themselves—and I probably wouldn't be allowed to discuss such sums with them if they did!

The next letter was written to my parents and they have sent it along for me to read, without comment.

"My dear friends, Mr. and Mrs. McCormick:

"I wonder if you would be broad-minded to read this letter, in the light of my writing it. It is fascinating to know that—many times, inspiration comes because of many reasons. When I say "inspiration"—I mean it with the thought of a beginning of a new life for one or more persons, who may be involved.

"This evening, I noted in the *Review-Journal*, this unusual article of a blonde fighting "bulls," and was struck with a favorable and sharp thought about your daughter. A 'plucky gal'—and, being interested in many things, was desirous of finding out—from you— WHEN SHE WAS BORN—*Month, day and year*.

"The Bible says: "Seek and ye shall find"—and if there is a possibility that her birthday components— would be perfect—she might be 'plucky' enough to marry me. When I say—'perfect'—I want you to realize that the human specie can be (—though rarely is—) matched up—PERFECTLY—as the four-legged specie— such as a dog for a dog, cat for a cat and so forth.

"Look about you, today, and note—HOW FEW—REAL MARRIAGES—there are. There are many legal arrangements—called—'marriages'—but in the true essence— and you know that I speak the truth—they are 'flops.'

"God—if you believe in him—WILLINGLY AND SINCERELY—always answers prayers—in many ways—and HE may be answering me. Time will tell. And—if the matching components are perfect—then she might be 'plucky' enough to have three children.

"I just leave this writing for your disposition, and repeat again:—Time will tell—. Thanks."

This is impossible for me to answer. Anyway, it was written to my parents. I may have sacrificed some of the freedoms of the North American girl, but I would still like to see a prospective husband and be consulted first. I'm afraid I'm not "plucky" enough for the above suggestion even if all my "components are perfect."

The next letter contains a clipping about my Tijuana fight from a Mexico City bullfight paper, written by a doctor who treated me. It is headlined that I merit the title of "heroine *torera*," and goes on to praise my fight. Well, he should; his bill was high enough.

There are the letters of faithful *aficionados*, bless them—*aficionados* from all walks of life. These mean much to me, and I enjoy speculating about those I have met and seeing how close I come to the truth when I do meet them.

Of course I meet many interesting people, too, as does anyone in public life—artists and writers and people of the theater. (After Tijuana I had a letter from Anne Miller in which she said she'd tried fighting bulls during a visit to Spain.) Writers seem to be the most curious about me—what makes me tick and why I want to be a bullfighter. Some of them, amateur psychiatrists, have interesting theories.

We took one writer from the West Coast with us as a member of my *cuadrilla* for my first fight after the Tijuana goring. I think he wanted to see if I could face the bulls again without stepping aside when the charge came. That fight was at Villa Acuña. I did get pushed around a bit by one of my bulls, but I did not get hurt— and I cut an ear, which I presented to the writer for his five-year-old son, who had watched me practice in Juárez. He already swings a mean cape—sort of in the manner of a *serpentina*. The writer was in the *callejón* with Martín, as assistant sword handler. I brought one bull right over in front of him for the *faena* and kill. He was much more worried than I was, though he was behind the barrier.

"Did you think I would be scared after Tijuana?" I asked him after the fight.

"I never doubted your courage," he said. "But I have seen brave men automatically give a little ground, against their will, after a grave goring. To most of us that is common sense, if you know you are likely to be hit. But I can understand your *pundonor*, and sensible or not, I take off my hat before such honor."

I have always been the type of person who can enjoy solitude. When I am at home in Juárez, a Saturday morning usually means doing just as I please. I think of all the things I should do—answering letters, budgeting, and the innumerable odds and ends that I usually do not get done. Nevertheless, even with the chores around the house I can daydream of how I can improve everything from fighting bulls to personal matters. I find this the best tonic for worrying, always searching for ways to lessen faults that are bothersome.

Sometimes Martín comes and we make it a point to find no work to be done with bullfighting equipment, and we take off in the car, or on foot, for the country. The last time we did this, I wore my *charro* hat. Martín swore I looked like a real *Mexicana*—until we stopped to buy a watermelon; then he told me to stay in the car because the vendor would take me for a tourist! That, for some reason unknown, led to an argument about the categories of different matadors. Finally I took my cape and practiced up and down the hot, dusty road—in bare feet, my pants rolled up just below my knees—until some *rancheros* stopped to rest and watch the curious spectacle.

Back home Martín cooked wonderful *enchiladas* while I played Bizet's *Carmen* on the phonograph and lay on the floor, reading a play by Sierra Martinez. A terrible mixture, because the play was pure humor and the opera, tragedy, but both were of Spanish background.

Another time when *El Oso* was away, we took the cape and went into the country to see if we could find stray cattle to try to stir up enough to have some fun. Finding the cattle was our problem, and we finally gave up and found some good music on my transoceanic port-able radio. When we got home, I thought of a pass I wanted to perfect and was trying it in the driveway when Alejandro drove up. He wanted to know why I was practicing in the evening; was I trying to become a lady wrestler? But when we went into the house, he talked for a long time about the difficulties of managing a successful bullfighter. I don't remember everything he said, but he did impress on me that someday the bulls would be easy for me. Just work and patience! And I thought how God had made the world and everything in it in seven days! Of course we don't know how long each day and night was. It was meat for meditation far into the night.

One Sunday, recently, when I had no fight, Alejandro and the family left early for a visit to friends in El Paso. As soon as they were out of the house, I got out Alejandro's *traje de luces* and donned the pants. Playing my *flamenco* records to my heart's content in the empty house, I practiced in front of the mirror, watching the different figures the tight pants helped to make, and the sequins glistening and shimmering with the movements in the light from the outside. I think how beautiful it would be to fight in *traje de luces!* Then I put on my Spanish leggings and shirt copied from the old days of Pepe Hillo. With *Carmen* going full blast, I think I fought twenty bulls in this getup, with the little Goya-type hat on half of the time. It was more fun than a picnic. (I hope there is no superstition about wearing Alejandro's pants.)

It has been a predicament that, as a professional woman bullfighter, I don't wear the *traje*, though I have dreamed of fighting in them since the age of seven. It is really a sacrifice not to wear them, but Alejandro thinks I would lose femininity if I did (though the best compliment is that I fought like a man). A bullfighter should not lose his or her own personality in the ring, and the construction of a woman makes the wearing of the traditional matador's costume more difficult. Mine is authentic, and not theatrical, at least. But I sometimes envy those who march with me into a plaza, their costume so fitting to the event. I keep looking in old books for illustrations of old costumes of Spain—so far with no luck so far as anything for me is concerned. But someday the plazas of Mexico, and other bullfighting countries, may see a strange suit of the past in front of the bulls. It will be authentic, and probably up to date in a sense, too.

Martín came to take me to see the *corrida* in the afternoon. It was easy to criticize the boys who were fighting large bulls, which were tricky. But I was humble in my judgments, remembering my fight in Juárez on Easter Day of this year, which was not good. I'd been nervous for a week beforehand and while the bulls started out well with the cape, they "pooped out" with the *muleta*. Alejandro was satisfied, but the public and I were not. I found out later that before the fight I'd given my flowers to the wrong Virgin again. I went to a church where all the images were covered because of Good Friday. A priest told a boy to take me to the one he said was Carmen, and I put my flowers at the feet of the shrouded image. When I went back after the fight I found it was not Carmen at all.

I redeemed myself later in Juárez in a hand-to-hand

match with a polished young *novillero*. I felt a little rebellious in this fight and did *desplantes*, such as kneeling in front of the bull, handling his horns, and so on. The public loved it. That can be vulgar, and I don't usually attempt it even when I think I can get away with it. It is a strange sensation to look a bull right in the face. I know that I am not afraid to do it even if I have to walk right up to the horns to learn his line of fight. This is not the same as recklessness, though some of the show-off familiarity with the bull may be.

Anyway, in this second Juárez fight this year, I cut ears and tails. That is the last fight I've had as I finish this story. It left a good taste in my mouth. There are several more scheduled, and there are proposals for a season in Portugal and one in South America. And there is Mexico City, when Alejandro thinks I am ready to fight there, that is something to look forward to!

But I spend little time thinking about the future. The present is always what we have, and the past is already gone. What lingers from the past is what we have learned from it when it was the present; the future is only the course and the goal on which we can set our sights. I think we may lose the present by not taking it as it comes. As it is for the long future, so I try to make it for the immediate future.

Thus if I lie awake the night before a fight I do not let myself think about the following day, other than to think how I can make it good for me. I do not project my thoughts ahead to what may be if I have a triumph or a failure. Of course I do not have complete control of my thoughts, but I do my best to guide them along constructive lines and then try to be willing to accept what comes, only regretting if I have not done my best.

Recently I arrived in a small town with my *cuadrilla* for a fight scheduled for the following day. It was raining pretty hard when we got there, and at supper there was some speculation as to whether or not a *corrida* could be held if the rain did not stop soon. There was the temptation to consider the possibilities, which I suppressed. It could be dangerous to hope one way or the other about it. I awoke at five in the morning and it was still raining, and there was quite a wind. Before I could control it, I thought that now I could relax and go back to sleep! The rain would erase the tension with the *corrida*. Then I thought about the specially selected bulls I'd miss, and before I knew it I was torn between desire to go back to sleep with assurance I would not fight and the worry lest the fight be postponed and I wouldn't have two of those bulls behind me.

Later I heard Mariano whistling *"La Macarena"* in the next room, and took it as a tip to get up and dress. It stopped raining after breakfast and I went back to my room for the always-scheduled "rest" before a fight. I went to sleep and awakened later in a sweat. Someone was pounding on the door. It was only the hotel man saying that someone was on the phone. It was the other fighter scheduled for the afternoon, calling from a town down the road to ask if the fight would be held. I said I didn't know but that I was getting ready. He said he doubted he could make it; the road was gullied by the rain and the buses were running late. Back in my room I thought how wonderful if he didn't arrive and I had four fine bulls to myself! That would help to compensate for the good bull I didn't get in Tijuana. By the time I had finished dressing, Alejandro came in to say the ring was like a fish pond. No fight.

So we all went down to eat *cabrito!* I sat at the head of the table with the picadors at the other end. (Often the matador does not eat with his *cuadrilla,* or only with his *banderilleros.*) Everyone was in good spirits, though we had missed a fight. I say little on such occasions; in Mexico it is more dignified for a lady to be attentive but not talk too much. But I have no difficulty listening to the experiences of these men—Mariano, who was a *banderillero* with the immortal Joselito and many other famous matadors; and Pancho Balderas, who was confidential *banderillero* to his famous matador brother, Alberto, and who was with him when he was killed in the ring trying to take a bull away from another matador. But the things they speak of when we are together are the interesting and humorous occurrences in the lives of bullfighters.

Today what thrills and inspires me is their account of a great festival recently held in Mexico City. That must have been a day for history! And hearing of it, I couldn't help thinking ahead and aspiring more than ever to be a supreme artist, forgetting the road to such a goal. In this festival the great, retired matadors, Pepe Ortiz, Heriberto Garcia, Jesús Solorzano, Paco Gorraez, Silverio Perez, and, the youngest of them all, Carlos Arruza, fought for the benefit of a foundation and the family of the matador Ricardo Torres, who had been killed during the past year. Rodolfo Gaona and Juan Silveti were escorts of the señora, the wife of the president of the Republic, who was the patroness of the festival.

One by one the ex-matadors arrived at the plaza to be greeted by old *aficionados,* newsmen, and cameramen, some of whom, it was said, wept and kissed the hands of the matadors. Before the time for the fight the stands started chanting: "Ortiz! Ortiz!" A procession of small boys went out and presented him with garlands of flowers, and when he fought he did again his famous *"quite* of gold," which he first performed in a competition with the best matadors of Spain, winning the trophy with this pass alone.

Jesús Solorzano, at the end of his fine performance, took the leather wine bottle someone threw down to him, and turning to the first lady of the country bowed and extended the *bota,* letting the thin stream of wine flow to his lips without spilling a drop. Then he capped it and accurately threw it back to the one in the stands who had tossed it down. He bowed again to her with gallantry when the garlands of flowers were presented to him. Each of the others in his own way acknowledged her, so that the people left the plaza speaking as much of the chivalry as of the great performances.

Mariano said Solorzano fought with "the hand from his heart." Each did well. I cannot recount the glowing words of my two *banderilleros,* who have seen all the great figures of the last years. I wish you could see Pancho demonstrate the stupendous pass with which Arruza commenced his *faena.* It baffles description.

To such men I offer my homage; they have kept alive the art to which I am dedicated, and they continue to offer inspiration for those who would follow in their footsteps. Hearing about them from my *banderilleros* is a rich experience, too, for in such contacts

I find background for my beliefs and way of fighting.

No! The world of a bullfighter need not be dreary. There is too much in it, even though he does not mix too much with crowds and society while he is fighting. If anything, such experiences as hearing of the benefit in Mexico City tend to make me dream too much of the future or of the past days of such matadors, whom I idolize. But they make the sweat and grind of practice and the "blood and sand" of *corridas* worth every hardship, bump, bruise, and wound.

Of course the future cannot be wholly put from my mind. A good bullfighter thinks of fighting indefinitely; he does not start counting the years to his retirement as an office clerk may do. He does what he does because he believes in it and in himself—in the spiritual and physical satisfaction that comes from his art. Death is with him but death is not an obsession. Life is as sweet to the bullfighter as to anyone else—perhaps, at times, a little sweeter.

If I do dwell on what I shall do when I retire from fighting bulls professionally, I think of a ranch in the uplands of Mexico. I think of a small herd of fighting cows and bulls, and of *tientas* and bloodlines and fine, brave specimens shipped to plazas for younger fighters.

Marriage? I suppose I would like to have a family, someday. But I do not think of that. I know that when I finish fighting I will no longer be young. I may be scarred. Marriage is put from my mind, and in my occasional dreams of a ranch I think of a foreman directing the men after discussing affairs of the ranch with me, and not necessarily a husband. That too is future, too far from the present.

More in my thoughts are actual fighting and perfecting myself and my art and skill, rediscovering what masters before me discovered; growing in the present toward the ideal I carry like a flame inside me, trying to make each moment an hour of truth. This is the phrase bullfighters use for the moment of a fight when the matador goes in with the sword, honestly, offering the bull his best chance to kill the man.

With this piece of religion—and it is religion to me—I can work in the shadows of those gone before me, and my work becomes my sanctuary. So, like the wind in my hair, the water in my mouth, and the security of the ground beneath my feet, so will the bulls be to me someday: natural and *right*. And I shall fight with instinctive understanding of what I am doing and what I should do.